FAILURE IS IMPOSSIBLE
The Story of Susan B. Anthony

FAILURE IS IMPOSSIBLE
The Story of Susan B. Anthony

Lisa Frederiksen Bohannon

MORGAN
REYNOLDS
Publishers, Inc.

620 South Elm Street, Suite 223
Greensboro, North Carolina   27406
http://www.morganreynolds.com

FAILURE IS IMPOSSIBLE: THE STORY OF SUSAN B. ANTHONY

Copyright © 2002 by Lisa Frederiksen Bohannon

Library of Congress Cataloging-in-Publication Data

Bohannon, Lisa Frederiksen.
    Failure is impossible: the story of Susan B. Anthony / Lisa Frederiksen Bohannon.
      p. cm.
    Includes bibliographical references and index.
    ISBN 1-883846-77-3 (lib. bdg.)
      1. Anthony, Susan B. (Susan Brownell), 1820-1906--Juvenile literature. 2.
    Feminists--United States--Biography--Juvenile literature. 3. Suffragists--United
    States--Biography--Juvenile literature. 4. Women's rights--United
    States--History--Juvenile literature. 5. Women--Suffrage--United
    States--History--Juvenile literature. [1. Anthony, Susan B. (Susan Brownell), 1820-1906.
    2. Suffragists. 3. Women--Biography.] I. Title.

HQ1413.a55 B65 2001
305.42'092--dc21
[B]

                                                                    2001030502

Printed in the United States of America
First Edition

For David, Ryan, Madeline, Kevin,
and Abigail Bohannon, with love.

Contents

Susan Brownell Anthony in her eighties.
(Courtesy of the Library of Congress.)

Chapter One

A Quaker Upbringing

In 1831, eleven-year-old Susan B. Anthony worked alongside her three sisters, Guelma, Hannah, and Mary, helping their mother with the household chores. Endless hours of mending, cooking, gardening, sewing, and cleaning for the Anthony family and the eleven mill girls who boarded with them filled their days. Although they lived in a fine, two-storeyed home, and Susan's father, Daniel Anthony, was considered a good and fair husband, the strain and responsibility for seven pregnancies, six children, and managing a household that included eleven boarders were her mother's alone to bear. It had left Susan's mother, Lucy Read Anthony, a joyless, worn out woman. Over time, observing her mother's life made Susan B. Anthony "less eager to enter that condition herself and more eager to improve it for others."

One of the most time-consuming chores was meal preparation. In those days before refrigeration and grocery stores, it was a year-round activity. Butter and cheese came from Grandmother Anthony's farm. Easy-to-grow and store root crops, such as potatoes, turnips, beets, and carrots were the primary vegetables, and meats that could be smoked or salted, like pork, rounded out a meal. Bread was the main staple. The Anthony women baked twenty loaves at a time, taking most of the day to mix, knead, set to rise, knead again, set to rise, and finally to bake the family's bread.

There were always clothes to be made, mended, and washed. One load of laundry required about fifty gallons, or 400 pounds, of water for washing, boiling, and rinsing—all of which had to be carried in buckets by Susan and her sisters from the spring to the kitchen. Fortunately Susan had an extraordinary skill at sewing, a chore she loved.

Born on February 20, 1820, in Adams, Massachusetts, Susan Brownell Anthony (named for her Aunt Susannah Anthony Brownell) was the second of Lucy and Daniel Anthony's seven children to survive childbirth. There were twenty-three states in the union that year. In all twenty-three states, "common law" practices ruled that "the very being or legal existence of the woman is suspended during the marriage . . ." In other words, common law made wives the legal property of their husbands.

Luckily for Susan, her father was a Quaker, and her mother, though raised a Baptist, had agreed to the children's Quaker upbringing. Quakers did not practice

Susan B. Anthony was born in this farmhouse in Adams, Massachusetts.
(Courtesy of the Library of Congress.)

common law. Their religious practices centered on their belief in the Inner Light—God's voice within each individual's soul. Daniel and Lucy were deeply devoted to one another and to raising a close-knit, loving family. Susan's earliest memories were of the times she spent with her two sisters, Guelma, born in 1818, and Hannah, born in 1821. The three girls were each others' best friends. A stillborn child followed. Then came Daniel in 1824; Mary in 1827; Eliza in 1832 (who then died at the age of two of Scarlet Fever); and lastly, Jacob Merritt in 1834.

At the young age of four, Susan learned to read, as did many girls in the Quaker faith. She and her two sisters had been sent to stay with their Grandmother and Grandfather Anthony for six weeks as her mother approached the delivery of her fourth child. There, Susan, Hannah, and Guelma received long hours of lessons each day. The strain of the lessons, at a time when she also had whooping cough, was too much for young Susan. When she returned home, the first thing her mother noticed was that her eyes had crossed.

Excited to show her mother that she could read, Susan was confused when Lucy immediately put away the books and told her that she had the prettiest eyes she had ever seen. Not reading restored Susan's left eye to its normal position, but her right eye remained crossed. As she grew up, she became self-conscious of her crossed eye. Though others hardly noticed, Susan tried to hide it when photographed by posing her right profile.

In addition to chores, school was an equally important part of Susan's childhood. Daniel insisted that both his sons and his daughters receive an equal education. When the district schoolteacher refused to teach Susan long division because she was a girl, Daniel opened his own school. One of Susan's favorite teachers there was Mary Perkins. Mary Perkins was not Quaker, but she nonetheless shared the faith's views of women's importance. Susan and her sisters saw a new image of womanhood in Mary. She was independent and educated and held a position traditionally given to young men graduating from universities. She introduced Susan and the other students to poems and schoolbooks with pictures.

What little playtime she had, Susan was likely to spend out-of-doors or at her Grandmother and Grandfather Read's house. Grandmother Read doted on her grandchildren and indulged them with delicious foods and sweets, and Grandfather Read entertained them with stories of his days as a Revolutionary War soldier. The time Susan spent watching the sun set, pondering the workings of insect communities, picking wildflowers, catching snowflakes, or nursing wounded animals left her with a lifelong appreciation of nature and of being outside, regardless of the weather.

At the age of twelve, Susan and her sisters took over the running of the household when their mother became ill during her seventh pregnancy. They continued with many of these management duties for the next several years. In time, Susan realized that her life was as busy as that of the girls who worked in her father's cotton mill, but there was one distinct difference—the mill girls were paid for their work. They received $1.50 per six-day workweek, plus board.

Daniel believed that his daughters should be able to support themselves, and he encouraged them to teach, the only profession open to women at the time. At fifteen, Susan began teaching the younger children at her father's school during the summer. From there she went to Easton to teach a Quaker family for $1.00/week, plus board. Later, she taught in the district school for $1.50/week, plus board. Determined to give his daughters a higher education to improve their teaching opportunities, Daniel decided to send them to Miss Deborah Moulson's Seminary, a Quaker Boarding School for Females, near Philadelphia. In a letter to a friend, Daniel wrote, "What an absurd notion that women have not intellectual and moral faculties sufficient for anything but domestic concerns."

When Susan was seventeen, Daniel accompanied her on the journey to join her sister, Guelma, at Deborah Moulson's Seminary. Although traveling was routine for Daniel, who made frequent trips to Philadelphia to sell his cotton products, Susan found the trip to Miss Moulson's Seminary "epoch-making." They took every mode of transportation in common use at that time— horse-drawn cart, steamboat, ferry, canal boat, and stagecoach. But when the time came for her father to leave her, Susan's happiness vanished. "Oh, what pangs were felt, it seemed impossible for me to part with him," she later wrote in her diary. She felt a deep loneliness living away from her family for the first time in her life.

The course of study for Miss Moulson's Seminary students was extremely thorough. It included orthography (known then as the art or use of correct spelling), reading, writing, arithmetic, grammar, geography, astronomy, natural philosophy, chemistry, history, composition, and "improvement in morality." "Improvement in morality" and striving to please Miss Moulson caused Susan great anxiety and concern. She seemed to do nothing right. According to Miss Moulson, Susan "laughed too much, thought too little, and did not properly dot her 'i's.' " As a result of always falling short of Miss Moulson's expectations, Susan developed a profound sense of inferiority which plagued her for many years thereafter.

Life at Miss Moulson's Seminary did have its bright spots, however. Susan and the other students enjoyed occasional sleigh rides and field trips to Philadelphia's Academy of Arts and Sciences. Her childhood experiences observing nature heightened her enjoyment of her science classes, and in one letter to her parents, Susan described "the pleasure of viewing the dust from the wings of a butterfly" through a microscope. "Each minute particle appeared as large as a common fly," she exclaimed.

Susan also formed a few close friendships while at Miss Moulson's. She enjoyed spending time with one of her best friends, Lydia Mott, a student teacher who was the niece of Lucretia and James Mott. Lydia Mott and Susan would become lifelong friends and later work together in the temperance, abolitionist, women's rights, and suffragist movements.

When the school term ended in 1838, Daniel picked up his daughters and took them to Yearly Meeting in Philadelphia, which was considered a high note of every Quaker's life. Following Meeting, they stopped in Brooklyn for two nights to visit relatives and shop. These activities belied the huge financial hardships that had been brewing for Susan's family (and much of America) since the economic panic of 1837. Susan would soon learn that the cotton industry that had brought them such prosperity had now become their financial undoing.

Daniel had mentioned his financial troubles in his letters to Susan. Similar to hundreds of other factory, warehouse, and insurance brokerage owners, he had expanded his business to take advantage of the increased demand for cotton. But when the nation's economy collapsed and the panic of 1837 ensued, many people, including Susan's father, were financially overextended.

Daniel's high debts forced him to file for bankruptcy. It was a traumatic time for the Anthony family. It was also an awakening for Susan as she learned that everything her family owned legally belonged to her father and could be sold to pay off his business debts. The flour, tea, and sugar; the children's schoolbooks; the family Bible and dictionary; her mother's spectacles; underclothes; and even presents given to her mother could all be seized in the bankruptcy. Susan's uncle, Joshua Read, helped them by buying back everything the family wanted, or needed, to keep.

Chapter Two

Headmistress

After the bankruptcy sale, Susan and her family moved to the nearby village of Center Falls, New York, where Daniel became the postmaster. They settled into a tavern and soon began taking in boarders and travelers to help pay their rent. Susan worked harder than ever. Her diary entries recorded her tasks: "Did a large washing today . . . Baked 21 loaves of bread . . . Have been weaving for several days past, yesterday and today wove 3 yards."

Life in Center Falls did not consist entirely of work, however. Friends visited, and Susan and her sisters enjoyed quilting parties, buggy rides, and picnics. Susan's mother recalled this time as the happiest of her life. But, the bankruptcy meant an end to any further education for Susan and her older sister, Guelma, as the family could no longer afford the $125 annual tuition. Susan and Guelma had to either support themselves or get married.

Susan chose to become self-supporting. She took an assignment as the assistant teacher at Eunice Kenyon's Quaker Boarding School located in New Rochelle, New York. It was May of 1839, and Susan was nineteen years old. Guelma stayed behind in Center Falls to plan her wedding to Aaron McLean, a Presbyterian and the son of Daniel's former partner in the Battenville cotton mills. Aaron had been a childhood friend of both Susan and Guelma.

Guelma's decision was an emotional blow to Susan. The sisters had been extremely close and intensely loyal to one another. Guelma's pending marriage now left Susan feeling betrayed and lost. Susan coped with the situation in the same way that her mother dealt with painful feelings: She withdrew and would not speak of them. "My feelings are inexpressible, therefore I will not try to say any more in reference to them," she wrote.

In the meantime, Susan developed a friendship with Eunice Kenyon, the headmistress of the Boarding School. This was her first serious friendship with any-one outside of her family. Eunice and Susan enjoyed long walks and conversations together. Eunice encour-aged Susan to adopt her own style of teaching and left Susan in charge of the school when she went home for a holiday. Eunice's confidence in Susan's abilities greatly eased the feelings of inferiority that had plagued her since her term at Miss Moulson's Seminary.

The pupils at Miss Kenyon's school were young children and the atmosphere was far less oppressive than the one Susan had experienced at Miss Moulson's, although student discipline remained strict. When asked in an 1896 interview, "Did you ever whip any of your scholars?" Susan replied, "Oh, my yes! I whipped lots of them . . . In those days, we did not know any other way to control children. We believed in the goodness of not sparing the rod. As I got older I abolished whipping. If I couldn't manage a child I thought it my ignorance, my lack of ability as a teacher."

While in New Rochelle, Susan received a number of gentlemen callers and a few marriage proposals. Unlike most young women her age, however, Susan was not interested in marriage for the sake of marriage. She did not purposefully choose a single life, she simply never felt that she met the right man. Moreover, the education she had received allowed Susan to enjoy financial freedom working as a teacher. This was not the case for most women who were dependent on their fathers or husbands to provide that security for them.

Susan used Lucretia Mott's description of marriage when sending letters of congratulations to newly married couples. Lucretia had said, "In the true marriage relation, the independence of the husband & wife is equal, their dependence mutual and their obligation reciprocal." Without this equality, Susan saw no reason to get married.

When Susan went to live with her cousin Margaret Caldwell and her husband, Joseph, her negative view of marriage was only reinforced. During Susan's stay, Margaret became ill during her very difficult fourth pregnancy. Susan was more than willing to help nurse Margaret, but soon Joseph began directing Susan in all aspects of running the household, caring for Margaret, and seeing to the every need of their three children.

Through it all, Joseph behaved selfishly and never gave a thought to helping. Susan wrote to her mother about one incident: "Joseph had a headache the other day and Margaret remarked that she had had one for weeks. 'Oh,' said the husband [Joseph], 'mine is the real headache, genuine pain, yours is a sort of natural consequence.'" Shortly after childbirth, Margaret died. Shaken by the whole experience, Susan described it as "enough drawbacks to make a woman content to remain single."

At the end of summer 1839, Susan's term at Miss Kenyon's school ended, and she returned home to Center Falls. She attended Guelma and Aaron's wedding on September 19, 1839, and took a teaching position at the local district school. She continued her social life, enjoying picnics, outings to the neighboring villages, and long buggy rides with friends and young gentlemen callers. Susan also underwent surgery to correct her crossed eye, something that had contributed to her feelings of inferiority and self-consciousness. But when the doctor removed the bandages, Susan "found he [the doctor] had cut the muscle too much, and that threw the eye the other way."

In 1843, Susan's family went through another difficult time when the Easton Society of Friends disowned Daniel for his decision to rent the top floor of their tavern to a group of young people for community dances. Having joined the temperance movement while in Battenville, Daniel had continued his reform efforts when he moved his family to Center Falls. Temperance reformers worked to ban the drinking of alcohol because they believed it led to irresponsible behavior. Thus, the village's young people who wanted to dance, not drink, knew that Daniel's tavern would be free of alcoholic beverages.

Even though Quakers saw both dancing and drinking as distractions from the Inner Light, Daniel worried more about the evils of drinking than the evils of dancing. He agreed to the young people's request but remained firm in his convictions that neither Susan nor her sisters attend.

The Easton Society of Friends took swift action, claiming, "It is with great sorrow we have to disown Friend Anthony, for he has been one of the most exemplary members of the Society, but we can not condone such an offense as allowing a dancing school in his house." Daniel did not appeal their decision but did continue to attend Meeting. Observing her father's commitment to his ideals rather than to his Society's orthodoxy was a tremendous lesson for Susan. It furthered her confidence in her own right to question authority and to take a stand for what she thought was correct.

In the summer of 1845, Hannah, Susan's younger

sister, announced her plans to marry. Susan again felt great emotional pain, dreading the "loss" of another dear sister. One of Susan's friends, Caroline, noticed her sadness and wrote to Anthony: "You must miss the society of your sisters, especially Hannah, as you were together so much and confided everything to each other."

Susan then decided to join her parents when they moved to the farm they had purchased in Rochester, New York. The money used to buy the farm had actually come from Lucy's parents who had left her $10,000 at their death. To protect her inheritance from being seized to settle Daniel's bankruptcy, Lucy's brother, Joshua Read, made the actual purchase of the farm and held the title in his name. Not until 1848, when the New York Married Women's Property Law was passed, could Joshua sign over title of the farm to Lucy. Passage of that law allowed married women to own property in their own name for the first time. Lucy would finally have a legal claim to what had been rightfully hers all along.

Rochester, New York—the center of political activism at that time—was a thrilling change for Susan and her parents. The newly completed Erie Canal shortened travel time from Buffalo to Albany, the state's capital, to one week instead of three, making Rochester a convenient place to stay overnight on this journey.

The Rochester Society of Friends was a welcomed source of intellectual stimulation for the Anthonys as well. A much larger Society, numbering close to 600, many of its Friends were Hicksite Quakers, a reform group within the Quaker community dedicated to radical social reform, particularly abolition—the fight to abolish slavery.

The Anthony's farmhouse soon became a gathering place for many of the nation's leading temperance and abolition leaders. Many of those leaders also argued for religious freedom and women's rights. Susan enjoyed lively discussions with her family's guests, including such reformers as Frederick Douglass and Lucretia and James Mott.

Though energized by the ideals and reform movements surrounding her in Rochester, Susan nonetheless remained anxious to pursue her own path by the spring of 1846. She found her opportunity in Canajoharie, New York. Her Uncle Joshua Read used his considerable influence to secure for her the headmistress position of the "female department" at the prestigious Canajoharie Academy. At the age of twenty-six, Susan left for her post and entered a whole new world.

Canajoharie was a lovely village in upstate New York, built along the banks of the Mohawk River. A Mohawk Indian name, *Canajoharie* means "pot that washes itself." Susan boarded with her married cousin, Eleanor, who was Uncle Joshua's daughter. Canajoharie was not a Quaker settlement nor was Eleanor of the Quaker faith.

Susan blossomed in her new found freedom and independence. For the first time, she could spend all of her wages on herself. She poured over her cousin's copy of *Godey's Lady's Book* and abandoned all outward appearances of her Quaker upbringing when she purchased brightly colored, fashionable dresses, hats, shoes, and accessories.

Her confidence grew, and the homesickness Susan had experienced while at Miss Moulson's and Miss Kenyon's did not follow her to Canajoharie. Susan even quit using "thee" and "thou," which was common to Quakers, and styled her long hair in several intertwining braids, secured by a shell-comb, as was fashionable at the time.

The young gentlemen of the village found Susan quite attractive and several called on her to join them for carriage rides and picnics. After living in Canajoharie for some time, Susan went so far as to accept an invitation to attend her first dance. She liked it, but found it awkward at the same time. When she learned that rum was being consumed at dances, however, she became disillusioned. And, finally, when her escort for an evening drank too much, she decided that dances were not for her. "My fancy for attending dances is fully satiated. I certainly shall not attend another unless I can have a total abstinence man to accompany me, and not one whose highest delight is to make a fool of himself."

Susan took her headmistress duties at the Academy seriously. Boys were taught on one floor and girls on another. Her twenty-five female students ranged from "young ladies right down to little girls." Susan taught them reading, spelling, writing, composition, grammar, arithmetic, botany, philosophy, and history. She was lively with her students, taking them on field trips, playing games, and engaging them with her keen sense of humor. She continued to be strict but no longer felt the need to be the rigid authoritarian figure she had been in her previous teaching assignments. Her students' excellent performances on their quarterly oral exams further established Susan as Canajoharie's intelligent and extremely competent "Schoolmarm."

In spite of her successes, life at Canajoharie began to bore Susan. She had mastered the duties of headmistress and felt the need to find something new and intellectually stimulating. Susan admitted: "I am out of sorts with the world." She had read letters from her parents and youngest sister, Mary, describing their attendance at a women's rights meeting held in Rochester. Susan was struck by the fact that Daniel, Lucy, and Mary had all signed a document called the Declaration of Sentiments at the convention.

Dubbed "the Women's Bill of Rights," the Declaration of Sentiments had been the basis of discussion at the first Women's Rights Convention that was held in Seneca Falls, New York, on July 19-20, 1848. It had been the first convention of its kind. In the Declaration of Sentiments, the authors spelled out the status of women by listing the civil rights that were denied to them. These included the right to own property, go to college, work in the legal or medical professions, keep one's wages, have custody over one's children, or receive a quality elementary school education.

The fact that her friend Lydia's aunt, Lucretia Mott, was one of the five authors of the Declaration of Sentiments furthered Susan's interest, as did the twelve Resolutions attached to the Declaration. The Resolutions, written by Elizabeth Cady Stanton, outlined the course of action that the authors felt society must take in order for women to achieve civil rights equal to those enjoyed by men.

In 1848, however, Susan could not fathom any possible reason for the ninth Resolution. Others at the convention must have agreed, because the resolution, which called for women's suffrage, was only adopted by the attendees after Frederick Douglass spoke passionately in its favor. The other eleven resolutions had not faced that kind of opposition.

Though greatly roused by the idea of a women's rights movement, especially one endorsed by people very important to her, Susan was not convinced that it was necessary. She believed that if society could be rid of intemperance, then women's lives would be sufficiently improved. Searching for something to challenge her mind and resolve her unsettled feelings, Susan decided to focus on Canajoharie's big reform movement—temperance: the movement against alcohol.

Exposure to the women whose lives were gravely affected by intemperance gave Susan a new appreciation for the plight of women outside of the Quaker

Susan took an interest in social reform movements in her late twenties.
(Courtesy of the Library of Congress.)

community. Strict religious teachings and laws had stripped these women of all their civil rights. Bible passages, such as "The man shall rule over thee," were cited to justify domestic violence. And, as Susan had learned from her mother's own experiences, laws prohibited women from owning property. Susan was determined to help those wives whose lives were dominated by poverty, shame, and physical abuse because of their husbands' intemperance.

Raised as a Quaker, Susan was accustomed to speaking publicly and was soon chosen the "Presiding Sister" of the Canajoharie Chapter of the Daughters of Temperance. She immediately set to work. On March 2, 1849, Susan gave her first public speech, which proved to be a turning point in her life.

In her speech, Susan challenged the women in the audience to do more than simply declare their support for temperance. She asked them to join together and work to improve their lives, the lives of their children, and the welfare of their entire community. "If we say we love the cause and then sit down at our ease, surely do our actions speak the lie," she said. Susan would give this same message with the same fervor throughout her life—women must go beyond mere words and band together to take decisive action for change. Susan had finally found what she unknowingly had been searching for—involvement in a cause that met her deeper, more personal need to change the world for the better.

Chapter Three

Temperance Reform

Though energized by her reform activities, Susan was disillusioned with the teaching profession. She was frustrated with being paid one quarter of what the male headmaster at the Academy was paid and with the limitations to women within the teaching profession as a whole. She had grown weary of teaching and resentful of the time it took away from the reform movement that she had embraced.

Sensing Susan's weariness, Daniel and Lucy suggested that she take over their farm. Daniel had accepted a position as a life insurance salesman and was often away. Her parents thought that the move might give Susan a "respite from teaching" and help them as well. Susan welcomed their offer and left Canajoharie in the fall of 1849 amidst toasts at her farewell dinner to "the smartest woman that was now or ever in Canajoharie."

Upon returning home, Susan joined the Rochester

Chapter of the Daughters of Temperance and set about running the family farm, taking responsibility for planting, harvesting, and marketing. She thoroughly enjoyed the change and found her new life challenging. Soon, she was organizing suppers and fairs for temperance.

These gatherings became opportunities to spread the objectives of the temperance movement, solicit new members, and raise funds, as well. Susan traveled to neighboring towns to teach other women how to do the same things. She also began writing articles supporting the temperance movement. Once again, she was proving her phenomenal leadership and organizational skills and her ceaseless energy for work. These talents would soon become her trademark in the world of social reform.

The temperance movement gave Susan her first glimpse of the workings of the political and legal processes. Previously, people considered intemperance a sin, a moral failing. But temperance reformers began to agree that laws and politics played key roles in the way the liquor industry was organized and protected, which in turn greatly contributed to society's intemperance. Tavern owners, distillers, and distributors all had a financial interest in promoting the consumption of alcohol. They used their political clout to make sure their financial interests were legally protected. These lessons in the political and legal processes provided excellent training for women in the temperance movement, especially for Susan.

By 1850, two other reform movements attracted Susan's attention: women's rights and abolition. The women's rights movement was growing quickly, and in 1850, hosted its First National Women's Rights Convention in Worcester, Massachusetts. Susan read an account in the *New York Tribune* of Lucy Stone's speech. Stone was a Garrisonian abolitionist and a women's rights activist. Garrisonian abolitionists were named for William Lloyd Garrison, a fiery newspaper editor who argued for the immediate emancipation of all slaves.

Congress's passage of the Fugitive Slave Act of 1850 deepened Susan's interest in the abolitionist movement. This act made it legal for Southern slave owners to pursue and capture runaway slaves who had escaped to the North. Outraged by the federal government's action, Susan decided that she wanted to expand her reform efforts to include antislavery.

Susan was not one to simply join or tag along. She needed to know the deeply rooted arguments for both sides of an issue. Her Quaker upbringing had instilled in her the moral reasons to oppose slavery; now she was determined to understand the intellectual arguments as well.

Following another of her father's example, Susan began associated with both Quaker and Unitarian religious groups, though she would remain a lifelong member of the Rochester Society of Friends. As long as a religious group focused on the divine goodness in all human beings, accepted all human beings as equal, and urged every individual to do their part to improve society, Susan was willing to participate in their meetings or services. She once commented on her religious orientation: "I pray every single second of my life; not on my knees but with my work . . . Work and worship are one with me."

To learn more about the abolitionist movement, Susan read as much as she could and attended antislavery meetings. She read accounts of abolitionist activities in newspapers such as Horace Greeley's *New York Tribune*, Frederick Douglass's *North Star*, and William Lloyd Garrison's *The Liberator*. She was deeply moved by the passionate speeches and strong arguments of the movement's leaders, including Lucy Stone, Wendell Phillips, and Lucretia Mott. All were Garrisonian abolitionists and long-standing friends or acquaintances of either Susan or her parents.

Susan found these reformers' commitment and political wisdom inspiring. She was particularly fond of their fervent, radical activism which she found in keeping with her own. William Lloyd Garrison argued for the immediate end to slavery: "Shall I tell a man whose house is on fire to give a moderate alarm; tell him moderately to rescue his wife from the hands of a ravisher; tell the mother gradually to extricate her babe from the fire into which it has fallen? . . . I am in earnest—I will not equivocate—I will not excuse—I will not retreat a single inch—and I will be heard!"

In 1851, Susan met Garrisonian abolitionists Abby

Kelley and Stephen Foster while they were in Rochester delivering antislavery lectures. Susan's intense interest in abolition impressed the Fosters, who invited her to accompany them as they continued their lecture tour through northern New York. Susan went along, but when invited to join them as a lecturer, she declined, convinced that she was not a skilled enough speaker to take on the lecture circuit.

Susan's heightened involvement in the antislavery movement, however, caused her to accept the invitation of her friend Amelia Bloomer to stay with her and attend an antislavery meeting in Seneca Falls, New York. Amelia Bloomer worked as the assistant clerk at the post office in Seneca Falls. Bloomer also published *The Lily*, a leading women's temperance newspaper in which several of Susan's temperance articles had appeared. Amelia was perhaps best known for promoting the radical style of women's clothing called "the bloomer costume" which consisted of ballooning trousers worn under knee-length skirts. Looking forward to hearing William Lloyd Garrison speak and secretly hoping to meet Elizabeth Cady Stanton, Susan traveled to Amelia Bloomer's home in May of 1851.

Susan and Elizabeth Cady Stanton met after the lecture, and Elizabeth later invited Susan to her home to meet with Lucy Stone and herself to brainstorm ideas for a People's College, their idea for the first co-educational college. Thrilled about the opportunity to become better acquainted with both women, Susan accepted. For Susan and Elizabeth, this marked the beginning of a lifetime of friendship and collaboration for social reform.

Susan was initially drawn to Elizabeth Cady Stanton by her powerful ideas and her disdain for the clergy who had considerable control over the temperance movement. Susan was also intrigued by Elizabeth's activities on behalf of women's rights. Five years older than Susan, Elizabeth had a vastly different upbringing. She had been raised in a wealthy family with parents who modeled the traditional views of girls and boys, women and men. She was also married and had given birth to four of her seven children by the time she met Susan. Elizabeth was overflowing with ideas but pinned down by her role as mother and wife. Susan did not have those responsibilities and possessed an energy of almost maniacal proportions. Their mutual respect and admiration would soon take them to new heights as leaders in the temperance, abolitionist, and women's rights movements. Together, they would become unstoppable.

Wanting to devote herself entirely to social reform, Susan made the decision to give up farming. She had saved some money from her teaching wages and her father was now able to provide some support. Financially secure, she planned to turn her energies to temperance reform full-time.

In 1852, Susan was elected to represent the Rochester Chapter of the Daughters of Temperance at the Sons

Susan B. Anthony and Elizabeth Cady Stanton (pictured here with her daughter Harriot) became best friends and worked together most of their lives to fight for women's rights. *(Courtesy of the Library of Congress.)*

of Temperance convention in Albany, New York. During the meeting, Susan rose to address the body and was pointedly ignored by the chairman. When she persisted, he thundered, "The sisters were not invited here to speak, but to listen and learn."

Outraged, Susan stormed out of the convention with other women delegates right behind her. The women already felt frustrated by the fact that the men in the movement insisted on separate organizations, but for them to invite women delegates and then deny them the right to actually participate seemed too much. Refusing to waste any more time overcoming the obstacles male reformers placed in the path of women reformers, Susan formed the Woman's State Temperance Society (WSTS) in January 1852.

The planners for the first WSTS convention agreed that men would be invited to attend, but they would not be allowed to vote or to hold office. In their first collaboration together, Elizabeth Cady Stanton set to work on the convention's opening speech, and Susan B. Anthony went to work organizing.

Susan wrote hundreds of letters, invited prominent people to speak, and arranged for posters and newspaper notices. She traveled from town to town raising money, recruiting members, and organizing new chapters. Additionally, influential men, such as Horace Greeley, William Henry Channing, Wendell Phillips, and William Lloyd Garrison supported Susan and Elizabeth's struggle for equality within the temperance movement, which broadened the support for the WSTS.

Susan's efforts paid off. When the convention opened on April 20, 1852, in the Corinthian Hall in Rochester, 500 of the more than 1,000 women and men who had joined the Society had made the trek. They elected Susan to serve as secretary, and she in turn requested that Elizabeth Cady Stanton serve as president.

In her acceptance speech, Elizabeth—dressed in a Bloomer Costume—wove the issue of divorce into her remarks, arguing that the law should not require a woman to remain the wife of a drunkard. Newspapers and churches went wild issuing scathing attacks on Elizabeth's suggestion that a woman had any right to divorce and that divorce had any relationship to temperance. Many WSTS members questioned Elizabeth's positions as well.

Undaunted by the attacks, Susan spent the summer canvassing the state for temperance. She worked to gather signatures on petitions to prohibit most retail sales of alcohol. That June, Susan and Amelia accepted the Men's State Temperance Society's invitation to attend their convention in Syracuse. They assumed that women were finally being accepted by the male society as equals. Instead, they were ignored and ridiculed in spite of having collected thousands of signatures on temperance petitions. Harassed as "a hybrid species, half man and half woman [in reference to their bloomer costumes], belonging to neither sex," they were forcibly escorted from the hall.

After that experience, Susan committed to the idea that until women obtained legal rights, men would not listen to their views. She later credited the temperance movement with turning her into a feminist, and in an 1895 interview recalled her reaction to one particular offense. At the close of a convention that Susan had worked very hard to organize, a resolution of thanks to various people, including Susan, was read. One man rose and moved that her name be stricken out as it was "unbecoming in a convention to thank a woman." Susan continued the interview: "I went home to my old Quaker father and said I had resolved that from that time on I would work for the cause of woman, and throwing myself upon my knees, I, sobbing, laid my head in my father's lap. He placed his hand on my head and gently said: 'If thee must, Susan, thee must.' "

In September 1852, Susan attended her first women's rights convention: the Third National Women's Rights Convention in Syracuse, New York. This convention proved to be another crucial landmark in Susan's career. With over 2,000 people in attendance, Susan was able to establish stronger connections and friendships with many of the movement's leaders, such as Lucretia Mott, Lucy Stone, Ernestine Rose, Gerrit Smith, Paulina Wright Davis, and Antoinette Brown Blackwell.

Though new at women's rights conventions, Susan was recognized for her leadership and commitment when she was appointed the convention's secretary. Lucretia Mott was elected president. At fifty-nine years

Lucy Stone was known as the "greatest orator" of the women's rights movement.
(Courtesy of the Library of Congress.)

of age, Lucretia would be known as the movement's "moral guide." Lucy Stone would be known as the movement's "greatest orator." Both Lucretia and Lucy would soon become two of Susan's closest friends, offering advice and encouragement in her early career.

When the third convention came to order, Susan B. Anthony read aloud the message prepared by her friend Elizabeth Cady Stanton, who at eight months pregnant could not attend. In her speech, Elizabeth asked how a government that taxed women could prohibit them from owning property or voting. Elizabeth demanded that women be admitted to the same jobs as men and condemned the church's teachings of a woman's inferiority and duty to serve her father and husband.

Public reactions were swift and negative. Even within the movement, many women felt uncomfortable with an attack on the church. This only strengthened Susan's growing belief that "the right which woman needed above every other, the one indeed which would secure to her all others, was the right of suffrage."

When the First Annual Woman's State Temperance Society's convention opened in 1852 in Syracuse, New York, Elizabeth and Susan attempted to make peace with those who were disturbed and angered by their linking temperance with women's rights. They succumbed to pressure and agreed to allow men to vote and hold office. Immediately following this concession, the group reorganized, changed the name to "The People's League," and voted Elizabeth out of office.

Susan was reelected as secretary but declined to serve.

To be treated thus after eighteen months of long, hard work angered Susan. But her friend Elizabeth begged her to "let the past be past, and to waste no powder on the Woman's State Temperance Society. We have other and bigger fish to fry." Together, they left the temperance movement and transferred their energies to the fight for women's rights and the abolition of slavery.

Chapter Four

Women's Rights and Abolition

Upon leaving the temperance movement, Susan was struck by the fact that many of the local groups that she had organized had folded almost as quickly as they had formed. She wrote in her journal: "Thus as I passed from town to town was I made to feel the great evil of woman's entire dependency upon man . . . Woman must have a purse of her own, & how can this be, so long as the wife is denied the right to her individual & joint earnings . . . there was no true freedom for woman without the possession of all her property rights."

In late 1853, Susan and Elizabeth began their campaign to increase the property rights of married women in New York. The Married Women's Property Act had been weakened by lawmakers since the original legislation was passed in 1848. Susan and Elizabeth divided the work in a manner that would be typical of their relationship over the next seven years: Elizabeth prepared an address that would later be presented to New

York's Legislature, and Susan set to work in the field gathering support for their cause.

Organizing some sixty volunteers, Susan and her helpers set out during the harsh winter of 1853-54 to gather signatures on petitions. Susan would choose to travel during the winter for most of her reform career. Because the harsh weather kept farmers from work—as well as keeping competing speakers at home—Susan was able to pull in large audiences to hear her appeals.

When lectures did not work, Susan and her volunteers went door-to-door. But in 1853-54, gathering support for petitions urging women's property rights and suffrage was a struggle. People were not ready to support a married woman's right to inherit her husband's property, let alone support her right to vote. In spite of the resistance, Susan and her volunteers collected 6,000 signatures demanding legislation to expand the existing Married Women's Property Act. They also collected 4,000 signatures supporting a woman's right to vote.

In February 1854, Elizabeth and Susan were ready to present their address and petitions to the state legislature. All their work fell on deaf ears. One legislator's response summed up the overall reaction: "We know that God created man as the representative of the race; that after his creation the Creator took from his side the material for woman's creation; and that by the institution of matrimony, woman was restored to the side of man, and that they became one flesh and one being, he being the head."

Susan and Elizabeth left the legislative session without any changes made in the law, but they were not discouraged. They would fight this same battle every year until the expanded Married Women's Property Act finally passed in March 1860. As was typical, instead of railing against the situation, they learned from it.

Susan decided the only hope for making changes in women's rights would have to come from a large movement comprised of women themselves. It was now obvious that men would not listen to a handful of reformers. Susan presented the idea that an effective women's rights movement needed a permanent, functioning organization with a large and stable membership.

Susan wanted to form a state convention of delegates representing local women's groups. She believed such a show of strength would greatly improve their chances of getting men to listen. If the wives, mothers, and sisters of the men in power supported women's rights, then would they not be able to convince those men of the need for women's rights as well?

On Christmas Day 1854, Susan set out for a five-month tour of fifty-four counties to take the movement to the women of New York. She stopped first in the town of Mayville, where she spoke to a small audience who had gathered in the courthouse. Susan lit the room with four pounds of candles that she had purchased for fifty-six cents. Her father had guaranteed payment for her lecture tour so that she could borrow several hundreds of dollars to print handbills.

Mayville was just the beginning of her long, grueling trip. The inns where she stayed did not have hot running water, nor were the rooms heated. Susan often had to break the ice in her water pitcher before she could wash up. But gathering signatures on petitions, spreading the ideals of the women's rights movement, and attracting new women to the cause was worth all the discomfort to Susan.

For the next five years, Susan took on the brunt of the fieldwork. Elizabeth's growing family kept her at home. By 1854, she had five children and would eventually have two more. The duties of motherhood and marriage plagued many of the leaders of the women's rights movement and quite often left the unmarried Susan as its driving force throughout the 1850s. Susan was greatly disheartened and angered when Lucy Stone announced her marriage plans in 1855. Antoinette Brown Blackwell followed suit in 1856. Susan felt they were abandoning the cause and found herself drawn closer to Lydia Mott, who was also unmarried.

In 1854, Susan received an invitation from Ernestine Rose, another prominent women's rights activist, to accompany her on a women's rights lecture tour. They began their tour in Washington, D. C. This would be Susan's first visit to the nation's capital. She found the tours of Capitol Hill, the White House, and Mount Vernon interesting. She was deeply moved when she viewed the original Constitution and Declaration of Independence. But as they continued the tour into several Southern cities, Susan was shocked to witness the horrors of slavery for the first time. She returned home more committed than ever to doing her part for the antislavery cause.

Two years later, she accepted the invitation of the American Anti-Slavery Society (AASS) to become one of its agents. This was Susan's first experience working closely with men. She looked forward to sharing ideals and strategies with the male leaders she admired, such as William Lloyd Garrison and Wendell Phillips. These two, and many of the others, became her mentors, inspiring her lectures and opening new doors. They, in turn, respected Susan for her intelligence, organizational skills, and forthrightness.

To fulfill her AASS duties, Susan organized a small army of speakers. She arranged their transportation, mapped out their routes, hired meeting halls, and coordinated advance publicity for their lectures. At the same time, she also maintained a grueling lecture schedule for herself. In 1857, Susan delivered one of her most memorable antislavery speeches, titled "What Is American Slavery?" Susan offered two answers to her question:

> It is the depriving of four million of native born citizens of these United States of their inalienable right to life, liberty, and the pursuit of happiness. It is the robbing of every sixth man, woman and child, of this glorious republic, of their God-given right—the

ownership and control of their own persons, to the earning of their own hands and brains, to the exercise of their own consciences and wills, to the possession and enjoyment of their own homes . . ."

Susan wrote this speech to protest the Dred Scott decision. Dred Scott was a slave who had gone to court to sue for his freedom. The Supreme Court had ruled that he could not sue because he was property, not a citizen, and thus had "no rights which any white man was bound to respect." Susan immediately saw the parallel between a slave's rights and a woman's rights. As William Lloyd Garrison had stated in 1840, "All of the slaves are not men."

In spite of great harm to her health—exhaustion and severe back strain—Susan continued her grueling drive for the combined reform efforts of women's rights and abolition. While traveling as an AASS agent, Susan also presented resolutions at teachers conventions. Susan had given one of her most memorable speeches regarding women teachers at the August 1853 State Teachers' Convention in Rochester. She had said:

"It seems to me, gentlemen, that none of you quite comprehend the cause of the disrespect of which you complain. Do you not see that so long as society says a woman is incompetent to be a lawyer, minister, or doctor, but has ample ability to be a teacher, that every man of you who chooses this profession tacitly acknowledges that he has no more brains than a woman?"

Susan was also the principal organizer for the Seventh, Eighth, and Ninth National Women's Rights Conventions. Her unstoppable energy, oratory capabilities, and organizational and fundraising skills soon caused Susan B. Anthony to become known as the "Napoleon" of the women's rights movement, a reference to the French emperor.

In 1858, Susan received word from Wendell Phillips that she had been named one of the trustees of the Jackson Fund. This fund was organized by Francis Jackson, a wealthy abolitionist whose daughter was stuck in a terrible marriage. Jackson wanted to fund the efforts of the women's rights movement in hopes of helping others in similar situations. Charles F. Hovey followed suit in 1859 when he established a $50,000 trust fund to benefit both the antislavery and women's rights movements. Small donations from men and women nationwide also remained forthcoming. All of these donations lent credibility and much needed financial support to the women's rights movement.

In 1859, Susan's winter lecture tour was cut short by the actions of a militant abolitionist named John Brown. Brown, a friend of Susan's family, led an attack on the Federal arsenal at Harpers Ferry, Virginia. He had intended to give the guns stored there to local slaves and to lead a slave revolt across the South. He was caught

Abolitionist John Brown was hanged after his raid on the arsenal at Harper's Ferry, Virginia. *(Courtesy of the Library of Congress.)*

and hanged on December 2, 1859, but when news of the raid travelled north and south, the fight over slavery intensified.

Though opposed to Brown's militant tactics, Susan was sympathetic towards his courage and willingness to act on his beliefs. To honor him, Susan held a memorial for John Brown in Rochester. She bravely sold tickets to the event from door-to-door and then gave the proceeds to John Brown's widow, Mrs. Mary Brown, and their children.

After John Brown's execution, Susan carried on with her winter lectures for AASS. She also continued to lobby on behalf of the expanded Married Women's

Property Law and to organize the Tenth National Women's Rights Convention—the last convention before the Civil War. By the time of that convention in May 1860, Elizabeth Cady Stanton was ready to resume her public appearances.

Elizabeth returned in full force. Her convention speech rocked the attendees as she launched an all-out attack on marriage. She offered ten resolutions recommending that New York's divorce laws be changed to make marriage nothing more than a legal contract that could be ended by either party in cases of drunkenness, desertion, or cruelty. In a state where the only legal ground for divorce was adultery, her proposal was radical.

Immediately, Antoinette Brown Blackwell offered thirteen resolutions to oppose Elizabeth's ten. Lucy Stone tried to keep the issue of divorce off the agenda. Susan rose to her friend's defense, offering an eloquent speech, agreeing that "from the time of Moses down to the present day, woman has never been thought of other than as a piece of property, to be disposed of at the will and pleasure of man."

Lucy Stone and Antoinette Brown Blackwell opposed the expansion of the women's rights platform to include divorce. Both Susan and Lucretia Mott supported Elizabeth, who believed that "the marriage question lies at the very foundation of all progress." A split within the movement's leadership began to take root.

Many of Elizabeth and Susan's male supporters be-

After John Brown's execution, Susan raised money for his widow, Mrs. Mary Brown.
(Courtesy of the Library of Congress.)

gan to attack them as well. Horace Greeley used his *New York Tribune* to level his criticism. Wendell Phillips attempted to censure Elizabeth's resolutions on marriage from the minutes of the convention, and William Lloyd Garrison met the resolutions with a cold silence.

Susan's actions during December 1860 furthered the hostilities. The wife of a Massachusetts state senator had sought Susan's help after her abusive husband had seized her property, locked her in an asylum, and refused to allow her to see her three children when she threatened to expose his adulterous relationships. In desperation, the woman took her thirteen-year-old daughter and fled to safety with Susan's help. Refusing to disclose the woman's whereabouts, Susan was utterly dismayed when both Phillips and Garrison urged her to do so for the "good of the cause." They argued that Massachusetts law gave custody of the children to the husband. Susan admonished them for their hypocrisy: "You would die before you would deliver a slave to his master, and I will die before I will give up that child to its father."

Chapter Five

Civil War and Reconstruction

The focus of Susan's reform efforts changed after the election of Republican Abraham Lincoln to the presidency. Seven Southern states then withdrew from the Union to form the Confederate States of America. Two months later, the Confederate Army opened fire on Fort Sumter, South Carolina, on April 12, 1861, and four more states left the Union. The Civil War had begun. It seemed as if securing equal rights for all women would depend on the success of abolition.

That year, Susan organized a "No Compromise with Slaveholders" tour of New York state in an effort to gather enough support to force President Lincoln to commit himself to full emancipation. Previously, Lincoln had publicly denounced the expansion of slavery in the new territories, but he had not wanted to tackle the question of full emancipation within the Union. Because of the war, Susan gave up her dogged pursuit of woman's suffrage. She had tried to schedule the Eleventh National Women's Rights Convention, but canceled it when her colleagues insisted that pursuing women's rights could hurt the Union cause. Additionally, many women had very little time to spare as they stepped in to fill the jobs and take on the responsibilities of the men who went to war.

Susan's "No Compromise" lecture tour was a gutsy move given the growing, equally active, pro-slavery countermovement. Susan assembled what she referred to as a "tremendous force of speakers," including Lucretia Mott, Gerrit Smith, Frederick Douglass, Stephen Foster, and of course, her friend Elizabeth Cady Stanton.

Susan and her fellow speakers encountered angry members of the countermovement on the tour. The mobs acted more violently than ever because many Northerners were placing the blame for the national crisis on the actions of the abolitionists. Newspapers viciously attacked Susan. She was threatened with guns and burned in effigy. Once an angry protester threw acid at her, which missed her face and instead burnt holes in her skirt. The tour eventually came to be known as the "Winter of Mobs."

Never backing down, even after war had been declared, Susan's uncompromising zeal kept her going. "What will you do with the Negroes [if freed]?" someone asked. Susan responded:

Do with them precisely what you would do with the Irish, the Scotch, and the Germans—Educate them. Welcome them to all the blessings of our free institu-

tions;—to our schools & churches, to every department of industry, trade & art. Do with the Negroes?
What arrogance in us to put the question, what shall
we do with a race of men and women who have fed,
clothed and supported both themselves and their
oppressors for centuries.

During the same year, Susan returned home for the
first time in over a decade. She wanted to spend time
with her family and work on the farm. One of her diary
entries read: "[S]uperintended the plowing of the or-
chard . . . The last load of hay is in the barn; all in capital
order. Fitted out fugitive slave for Canada with help of
Harriett Tubman." Returning home was a fortunate decision, for in November 1862, Susan's father died of
"neuralgia of the stomach."

Daniel Anthony had voted for the first time in his
life in 1860, casting a ballot for Abraham Lincoln. He
was convinced that only war could bring an end to
slavery, a heavy decision for a Quaker committed to
nonviolence. A letter Susan wrote, dated January 22,
1875, describes the impact her father's death had on
her: "[I]t seemed to me the world and everybody in it
must stop—It was months before I could recover myself—and at last it came to me; that the best way I could
prove my love & respect for his memory, was to try to
do more & better work for humanity than ever before."
Susan continued her fight to end slavery as she mourned
her father's death.

In September 1862, President Lincoln announced that all slaves in the Confederate states "shall be then, thenceforward, and forever free," as of January 1, 1863. Many abolitionists found cause to celebrate over the Emancipation Proclamation. For Susan B. Anthony, Elizabeth Cady Stanton, Wendell Phillips, and other like-minded, Garrisonian abolitionists, however, the Proclamation did not go far enough. What about the slaves in Union-occupied states? Also, what good did emancipation do in Confederate-occupied states without a Federal government to enforce it?

To settle the question once and for all, Susan and Elizabeth formed the Women's National Loyal League (WNLL) in 1863. It was the first women's political organization, and it received the strong support of male Republican leaders and fellow male abolitionists. WNLL's objective was to press for an amendment to the Constitution to abolish slavery altogether.

In her opening speech at WNLL's first meeting, Susan B. Anthony urged people, including the "President, Congress, Cabinet and every military commander," to acknowledge that slavery was the true cause of the war. She concluded by saying, "Forget conventionalisms; forget what the world will say, whether you are in your place or out of your place; think your best thoughts, speak your best words, do your best works, looking only to suffering humanity, your own conscience, and God for approval."

The hard feelings that arose between Susan and influential male leaders over Elizabeth Cady Stanton's ideas on divorce were temporarily put aside for abolition. Editor Horace Greeley showed his support for the WNLL and its objective to pass a Thirteenth Amendment to end slavery in the *New York Tribune*. Susan and Elizabeth's longtime friend Wendell Phillips, the newly installed leader of the American Anti-Slavery Society, used the AASS's *National Anti-Slavery Standard* to publish notices and articles created by Susan and Elizabeth. Theodore Tilton, editor of the *New York Independent*, a liberal Congregational newspaper, joined Phillips and Greeley in supporting the WNLL. With such influential support, the WNLL was able to achieve great things.

Under Susan and Elizabeth's leadership, the WNLL grew to 5,000 members and gathered 400,000 signatures on petitions that urged Congress to pass a Thirteenth Amendment. It was a monumental success and the largest petition campaign in history at that time. Susan supervised 2,000 volunteers nationwide on an extremely tight budget. Her expense log recorded a typical lunch on the road at that time of "milk, strawberries, and two tea rusks" for thirteen cents.

Receiving Senate approval in April 1864 and House of Representatives approval in January 1865, the Thirteenth Amendment was ratified by the states in December 1865, only months after the Civil War ended. Slaves finally appeared to be free. But, almost immediately Southern states began passing laws, known as "black codes," to keep former slaves from voting, testifying against whites in court, serving on juries, or joining the militia. The Ku Klux Klan formed in 1866, calling themselves the ghosts of Confederate soldiers, and terrorizing freed slaves and anyone who helped them.

The assassination of President Abraham Lincoln in April 1865 stunned the nation and dampened the hopes of social reformers. Andrew Johnson, a Democrat from Tennessee, became president. Johnson pardoned former Confederate officials and army officers, which left them eligible to run for office and vote. The year 1865 saw four former Confederate generals, six former Confederate cabinet members, fifty-eight former Confederate congressmen, and the former Confederate vice president take seats in Congress. Those Democrats and others of like mind made up one side of the post-Civil War Reconstruction effort, intent on promoting white supremacy.

On the other side of the Reconstruction effort were the "Radical Republicans," progressive members of Congress who wanted the South to accept the end of slavery. They also saw the potential for an increased number of Republican Congressional seats if they succeeded in getting African-American suffrage. To accomplish their objectives, Radical Republicans drafted a Fourteenth Amendment "to protect the rights of all male citizens, regardless of race or color."

Susan was in Kansas at the time of the amendment's proposal. She had gone there to visit her brother Daniel during the final weeks of the war and then stayed to organize "freedmen's relief" for the huge numbers of emancipated slaves who had flooded into the state. Susan was shocked to see the word "male" included in the draft of the Fourteenth Amendment. Never before had a citizen been identified by gender in the Constitution. Alarmed that the Amendment would weaken women's claims to their rights as citizens, Susan returned to New York in late summer 1865 to join forces in protest with Elizabeth Cady Stanton.

Susan and Elizabeth drafted a petition for woman suffrage to present to Congress and in a few months were able to collect 10,000 signatures. However, they also collected a huge amount of resistance from many abolitionists and Radical Republicans who feared that including women's suffrage would make ratification of an already controversial Fourteenth Amendment even more difficult.

Believing they still had the support of Theodore Tilton, William Lloyd Garrison, Wendell Phillips, and other male leaders, Susan and Elizabeth discussed merging the antislavery and women's rights groups into one organization. This new organization would then fight for suffrage for both African Americans and women.

Phillips and Tilton seemed enthusiastic and agreed to present a resolution to that effect at the May 1866 National American Anti-Slavery Society (NAASS) Convention. Susan and Elizabeth planned to do the same at the upcoming Eleventh National Women's Rights Convention—the same convention that Susan had cancelled at the start of the war.

When Susan and Elizabeth learned that the resolution had not been included on the NAASS agenda, they felt deeply betrayed. Determined that their colleagues' betrayal would not jeopardize the formation of the new organization, Susan proposed the resolution just days later at the Eleventh National Women's Rights Convention on May 10.

Many women's rights activists and abolitionists joined Susan and Elizabeth's cause, including Lucy Stone, Lucretia Mott, Antoinette Brown Blackwell, Lydia Mott, Sojourner Truth, Frederick Douglass, Parker Pillsbury, Theodore Tilton, Stephen Foster, and Ernestine Rose. The newly formed American Equal Rights Association (AERA) elected Lucretia Mott president. The group fought for universal suffrage.

Within a month of the formation of the AERA, however, Congress passed the Fourteenth Amendment and sent it on to the states for ratification. Disheartened but not beaten, the leaders of the AERA decided to take their efforts to the state level. Over the next several months, they labored to remove gender and race restrictions from the state constitutions in New York, Kansas, Maine, Massachusetts, Ohio, Missouri, and the District of Columbia.

Susan and Elizabeth chose to first concentrate their efforts in their homestate of New York, later working as AERA agents in Kansas. They were so intent on securing women's rights at whatever cost that they made some unfortunate decisions which would hurt them and the women's rights movement dearly. Their first mistake occurred at the New York Constitutional Convention. Susan, Elizabeth, and their volunteers had canvassed all sixty counties in the state gathering 28,000 petitions to remove the word "male" from the New York State Constitution. One of the signers was Mrs. Horace Greeley.

Horace Greeley had been siding with Republicans and other abolitionists who claimed that it was the "Negro's Hour." Americans coined the phrase the "Negro's Hour" to describe the idea that women should set aside their claims to equal rights and assist efforts to gain equal rights for freed, male African Americans. Greeley said,

> This is a critical period for the Republican party and the life of the Nation. The word 'white' in our Constitution at this hour has a significance which 'male' has not. It would be wise and magnanimous in you [women] to hold your claims, though just as imperative, I grant, in abeyance until the negro is safe beyond peradventure, and your turn will come next . . . this is 'the negro's hour.'

Unwilling to wait, Susan hoped that Mrs. Horace Greeley's signature on a petition presented to New York's Constitutional Convention would cause Mr. Greeley to change his stand. Not only did the delegates vote 125 to nineteen to reject the amendment at their mid-July 1867 Constitutional Convention, but Horace Greeley was so deeply embarrassed when his wife's name was read as one of the signers that he vowed to forever oppose Susan and Elizabeth's political efforts.

Discouraged, Susan and Elizabeth decided to accept the invitation of Kansas state Senator Samuel Wood, a Democrat, to join the fight for woman's suffrage in Kansas. Though Wood had voted against African-American suffrage every year since 1862, he proposed the addition of a woman's suffrage referendum to the already circulating African-American suffrage referendum.

Preceded by fellow AERA members Lucy Stone and her husband, Henry Blackwell, Susan and Elizabeth traveled the 1500 miles to Kansas in late August 1867 to work for Wood. In reality, Senator Wood was only pretending to support women's suffrage. He actually believed that by tagging women's suffrage to the African-American suffrage referendum, the latter would go down to defeat. Whom better to call on to draw support for women's suffrage than Susan B. Anthony and Elizabeth Cady Stanton?

Susan and Elizabeth threw themselves into the campaign for women's suffrage. Schoolhouses, barns, sawmills, and cabins became their lecture halls. Taking different routes to cover more territory, they traveled in freight trains, squeezing themselves between bags of flour and cases of shoes and tools. They rode twenty-five to thirty miles a day in lumber wagons and open buggies, crossing muddy, over-flowing rivers and streams in the snow and rain. For weeks at a time, they lived on hard biscuits, bacon, tinned meats, a few vegetables, and dried fruit.

Through it all, Susan's biggest complaint was the bedbug. After one four-day stay, Susan plucked bedbugs from her hair and the seams of her clothing and still found herself covered with bites. Nonetheless, Susan would keep this kind of rigorous traveling schedule for years to come. As the battle for suffrage moved west, Susan sometimes spoke in 200 different communities from the Atlantic to the Pacific in one year.

During their Kansas campaign, Susan and Elizabeth made the acquaintance of George Francis Train, as well as their second big mistake. Susan and Elizabeth both realized that they would need the support of both Democrats and Republicans if they were to secure women's suffrage. Thus, they were open to the ideas of George Francis Train, a Democrat, eccentric millionaire, and vocal advocate of women's suffrage. Train was also a racist.

Susan and Elizabeth chose to overlook Train's racism because he was the one person who offered to help when their abolitionist and Republican friends had abandoned women's suffrage in favor of the "Negro's hour." Train offered his help in the form of campaigning in Kansas and financing a newspaper that Susan and Elizabeth would own and operate.

In the end, both Kansas referendums went down in defeat at the polls in November 1867, although women's suffrage received 9,000 votes, which Susan found encouraging. She could not have imagined at the time that it would take another fifty years and 480 campaigns to urge legislatures to submit suffrage amendments to voters; forty-seven campaigns to induce state constitutional conventions to write women's suffrage into state constitutions; 277 campaigns to persuade state party conventions to include women's suffrage planks; thirty campaigns to urge presidential party conventions to adopt women's suffrage planks in party platforms; nineteen campaigns with nineteen successive Congresses; and hundreds of women's lifetimes, hundreds of thousands of women's volunteer hours, and millions of dollars from small donations before women convinced men to vote to remove the word "male" from the Constitution.

Chapter Six

The Women's Rights Movement Divides

Convinced that a newspaper of its own was what the women's rights movement needed, Susan and Elizabeth readily accepted financial help from the notorious George Francis Train. Lucy Stone could not believe the initial reports of this arrangement. Other AERA Republicans and abolitionists were equally shocked to learn that Susan and Elizabeth had partnered with Train, a self-proclaimed racist. Ignoring their animosity, Susan and Elizabeth published the first issue of their newspaper, *The Revolution*, on January 8, 1868. Susan became the proprietor and manager, while Elizabeth worked as an editor.

In addition to suffrage articles, Susan and Elizabeth published articles on divorce, dress reform, and prostitution in the sixteen-page weekly newspaper. They explored the horrible conditions of working women and discussed women's labor unions and eight-hour workdays. Though its influence spread far, *The Revolution* lacked money. George Francis Train's financial backing lasted only a short time. Investors were leery of the controversial paper, and Susan and Elizabeth limited advertising to only those products they could personally endorse. Their newspaper soon fell into financial trouble.

In the meantime, the problems caused by their association with George Francis Train and their fallouts with Horace Greeley and Wendell Phillips came to a head at the May 1868 meeting of the AERA. There, Susan introduced a resolution urging the association to oppose the Fourteenth Amendment and to resolve to work for women's suffrage only. Her resolution was soundly defeated. Animosities continued to mount.

In February 1869, Congress passed the Fifteenth Amendment as the final element of the Radical Republican's Reconstruction program. For Susan and Elizabeth, this was the final straw. Written to prevent states from prohibiting the right to vote on the basis of "race, color, or previous condition of servitude," the Fifteenth Amendment worried Susan and Elizabeth. They thought it would allow states to deny suffrage to other groups of citizens, especially women.

Susan and Elizabeth headed for the Midwest to fight the amendment's ratification. Lecturing in Illinois, Missouri, Wisconsin, and Ohio, they urged women to oppose the Fifteenth Amendment and instead support a proposal for the women's suffrage amendment that Elizabeth had written in 1868.

The schism that had been widening over the "Negro question" among the leaders of the AERA finally split at their May convention. The convention delegates were consumed by debate over support for the Fifteenth Amendment. Susan attempted to introduce Elizabeth's proposal for a women's suffrage amendment, though she was resoundingly defeated. In the end, the convention attendees almost unanimously adopted the Fifteenth Amendment and rejected any support for a woman's right to vote.

Furious, Susan and Elizabeth formed the National Woman Suffrage Association (NWSA). Elizabeth served as president, and Susan became a member of its executive committee. Lucretia Mott, Lydia Mott, and Martha Wright joined them. They hoped to defeat the Fifteenth Amendment and to obtain passage of a women's suffrage amendment.

That November, Lucy Stone led the remaining members of the AERA to organize the American Woman Suffrage Association (AWSA). Stating that it was the "Negro's hour" and that his needs were far greater than woman's, the AWSA would fight for passage of the Fifteenth Amendment and then seek women's suffrage on a state-by-state basis. Frederick Douglass, Wendell Phillips, Horace Greeley, Stephen and Abbey Kelley Foster, and Henry Blackwell joined Lucy. The women's rights movement would remain thus divided for the next twenty years, though Susan would make efforts towards reconciliation from time to time.

Susan B. Anthony celebrated her fiftieth birthday in 1870. The event was marked by a party in New York City. Susan's diary entry read: "Fiftieth birthday! One half-century done, one score of it hard labor for bettering humanity—temperance—emancipation—enfranchisement—oh, such a struggle!"

By the spring of that year, Susan and Elizabeth's beloved newspaper, *The Revolution*, was in debt for $10,000. The women decided to terminate publication. Susan B. Anthony gained high regards, even from her harshest critics, for taking on the sole responsibility for repayment of the debt. When asked why she did not declare bankruptcy, Susan said, "My pride for women, to say nothing of my conscience, says 'no.' " She repaid the debt within six years.

During that time, Susan earned money in part by going on a speaking tour of the Midwest. One hundred women of Lorain County, Ohio, presented Susan with an argument against women's suffrage:

> We feel that our present duties fill up the whole of our time and abilities . . . Our fathers and brothers love us. Our husbands are our choice and are one with us. Our sons are what we make of them. We are content that they represent us in the cornfield, the battlefield, at the ballot-box, and the jury box, and we them in the church, in the school-room, at the fireside, and at the cradle . . . we do, therefore respectfully protest against legislation to establish woman's suffrage in Ohio.

Susan went out of her way to be polite to the women who opposed suffrage. "Remonstrants," as they were called, were given her courteous respect. She even arranged on occasion to allow them time to speak their opposing views on the platform from which she, herself, spoke. Susan liked to remind them that without the women's rights movement, they would not have been allowed to speak publicly to the body of men gathered to hear their address.

Beginning with these suffrage tours, Susan saw the value of granting interviews as a means of spreading the suffrage message. She saw interviews as opportunities to put a positive spin on a negative suffrage event. She even created a press bureau within the suffrage association to ensure that the right "take" was given on any suffrage activity.

Susan's interviews had secondary importance, as well. They showed the nation the woman she really was. One reporter remarked, "I was entirely won by her genial manners and sunny spirit . . . there is a wonderful magnetism about the woman that draws and attracts irresistibly." In time, newspapers so desperately sought an interview with Susan or Elizabeth that any reporter gaining access to either woman experienced a career boost.

Susan mastered using the mail to spread the suffrage message. Her friend Anna Howard Shaw said of Susan: "She does not wait to be asked for it. She just sends it out in every letter she posts. When she pays her grocer's bill into the envelope go all the leaflets that one cent will carry . . . A letter of congratulations to the mother of a new baby has its freight of suffrage documents . . ."

In addition to interviews and the mail, Susan used congressional and state legislative records to spread the suffrage message. Once an item was submitted to a legislative body—whether it was a written petition, copy of a speech, letter, or oral testimony—its every word became part of the official record. Then, it was a public record available to be reprinted in newspapers or other publications.

Susan was quite successful at getting the suffrage message out, and she managed to be just as successful at raising funds for the cause. The secret of her fundraising success was the way she used her personal commitment to set an example for others. Susan gave every penny she earned or raised to the cause, keeping only a pittance to live on. In turn, she convinced others that they had a duty to sacrifice themselves for the cause as well. Day laborers sent in pennies, professionals sent in dollars, and wealthy philanthropists sent in huge donations. Comments such as, "I have done without tea this week to bring you this," and "I made a piece of fancy work evenings & sold it for this dollar," accompanied the proud donations of seamstresses and laundresses.

Women suffragists who could not afford to give cash gave of their time. After working a ten-hour day, women would stop by the suffrage office and take home armloads of circulars to address and fold at night. One newspaper reporter wrote of Susan's power to enlist the support of others: "She has carried on more campaigns upon less capital than ever did Napoleon or any other commander of whom record has been preserved."

January 1871 offered Susan, Elizabeth, and other NWSA activists the opportunity to attend the House judicial hearing to hear the address of a woman who had already created a stir: Victoria Woodhull. Susan had tried to interview Woodhull in early 1870 for *The Revolution.* A newspaper publisher and editor, the first woman stockbroker, and a women's rights activist, Victoria Woodhull was an intriguing figure.

In her address, Woodhull argued that the Fourteenth and Fifteenth Amendments already gave women, as citizens of the United States, the right to vote. Woodhull was not the first person to argue the "New Departure" strategy, as it was called, but she was the first person to demand that Congress acknowledge the legitimacy of the argument by enfranchising women. If the "New Departure" strategy worked, it eliminated the need for a constitutional amendment guaranteeing female suffrage.

The inner circle of the NWSA immediately welcomed Victoria Woodhull. They persuaded her to repeat her congressional address at their May convention. There, the members of NWSA embraced her "New Departure" strategy and left the convention charged to go to the polls and vote.

Deciding they would have better luck gathering support for woman suffrage in the Far West than with the "old fogies of the eastern states," Susan and Elizabeth left on a suffrage lecture tour together in June 1871. They traveled by train from Chicago to California, enjoying the magnificent scenery of the western states and the uninterrupted time together. Their suffrage campaign, however, barely survived Susan's defense of Laura Fair, a notorious prostitute, shortly after their arrival in San Francisco.

Susan was giving a speech in favor of women's suffrage and equal pay for women. Towards the end of her speech, Susan used a local figure as an example for her argument. She stated that Laura Fair would not be in jail for the murder of her lover, a prominent, married citizen of San Francisco, if women enjoyed the same economic freedom as men.

The crowd went wild condemning Susan—and so did the newspapers. They declared that she favored prostitution. Nothing could have been further from the truth. Susan abhorred it, but she equally abhorred society's double standard that allowed men to hire prostitutes but scandalized women for being prostitutes, a "profession" that was the only means of financial support for many women. The vehement attacks on Susan's speech marred their remaining California lectures.

Susan traveled on through Oregon and Washington after the California disaster, and Elizabeth returned to New York. One of Susan's "finer performances" occurred in Portland, Oregon, when she responded to the proclamation "WOMEN DO NOT WANT TO VOTE," saying: "I don't believe it . . . Then why do men put the words "white males" into their Constitutions? . . . Men don't fence a cornfield because the pigs don't want the corn, but because they, themselves, do. They fence the field to keep the pigs out."

Like so many of her lecture tours, this trip was long and grueling as described in her January 1872 diary entry: "on way home, Rochester N.Y., from six months in California, Oregon Wash. Ter. & Nevada—six months of constant Travel full 8000 miles—108 lectures—The *year's* work—full 13,000 miles travel—170 meetings."

Susan attributed her ability to work and sustain such a punishing travel schedule to the daily regime she followed. She woke up early, ate simple meals, did plenty of outdoor walking for exercise, refused to eat late evening dinners, drank absolutely no alcohol, and went to bed by nine or ten o'clock at night. A reporter remarked that "Miss Anthony . . . was generally one of the first down to breakfast in the hotel dining room, and, although there were all sorts of rich dishes on the bill of fare, she never failed to call instead for oatmeal, cracked wheat, or something of that kind." In addition to her daily regime, Susan credited "always being busy, never having time to think of myself, and never indulging in any form of self-absorption" for her tremendous energy.

During those rare times when Susan did take a rest from her hectic travel schedule, she enjoyed reading literature. Her favorite piece was Elizabeth Barret Browning's long poem, *Aurora Leigh*. Susan saw in Browning's character Aurora Leigh her own conception of a "true woman." Also, Susan spent free time visiting the home she shared with her mother and sister Mary at 17 Madison Street in Rochester, N.Y. Her sisters Guelma and Hannah and their respective families also lived in Rochester.

During the months preceding May 1872, Victoria Woodhull had become more and more controversial as rumors of her "free love" ideals, scandalous living arrangements, and questionable family background were published and circulated. Susan agreed with many of Woodhull's ideals, but she was deeply concerned that the negative press was hurting the suffragist movement. She warned the NWSA leaders and urged them to keep a distance. Yet, many, including Elizabeth, had continued their close relationships with Woodhull while Susan was on her western speaking tour.

Fearing the worst, Susan returned to the East. She arrived just in time to stop Woodhull's two attempts to take over the May 1872 NWSA convention for her own presidential aspirations. But, when Woodhull convened what she called her People's Party Convention at another hall nearby, Elizabeth and other NWSA members were present. Woodhull used that convention to form the Equal Rights Party and to nominate herself as the Party's presidential candidate. Susan felt deeply hurt by the actions of her friends, especially Elizabeth.

Woodhull's Equal Rights Party did not last long. Victoria Woodhull blamed the leaders of both the NWSA and the AWSA and the press for her failed presidential bid and retaliated by igniting a scandal. She published a complete "exposé" in her journal, *Woodhull and Claflin's Weekly*, of an alleged affair between the President of AWSA Henry Ward Beecher and the wife of newspaper editor Theodore Tilton. Woodhull cited leaders of NWSA for having known of and confirming the affair. Because the people involved in the allegations were from both sides of the women's rights movement, the press coverage linked the entire movement to Woodhull's "free-love" ideals and scandalous behaviors.

Shocked and dismayed by Woodhull's actions, Elizabeth Cady Stanton joined Susan in severing all ties with her. Susan wrote in her diary: "I never was so hurt by the folly of Stanton . . . Our movement as such is so demoralized by the letting go of the helm of the ship to Woodhull—though we rescued it—It was by a hair breadth escape." Their friendship survived the crisis. The impact on the women's rights movement, however, was not so easily repaired. The scandal and the subsequent Beecher-Tilton adultery trial would negatively impact membership in the NWSA and the AWSA and set back public support for woman suffrage throughout the mid-1870s.

Chapter Seven

Woman Suffrage above All Else!

The City of Rochester witnessed a first on November 1, 1872, when fifty women, ready to test the "New Departure" strategy, joined voter registration lines throughout the city. In line at the Eight Ward registration office were Susan B. Anthony, her three sisters, Mary, Guelma, and Hannah, and eleven other women. When the registration inspectors balked at the idea of registering them to vote, Susan read out loud the Fourteenth Amendment and the state election law. She pointed out that nothing in either of them expressly prohibited women from voting. The registration officers reluctantly agreed.

Susan returned with her sisters on election day, November 5, and cast her first and only presidential ballot of her life. She voted for Ulysses S. Grant, the Republican candidate, later declaring in a letter to Elizabeth, "Well I have been & gone & done it!"

Though Susan's bold actions made headlines for almost three weeks, the government waited until November 28 to do something about it. They arrested Susan B. Anthony on Thanksgiving Day, charging her with "voting without having a legal right to vote." Susan insisted that U.S. Marshall Keeney put her in handcuffs to take her downtown. He refused. She was released on bail paid by her attorney, and her trial was set for the following June.

Susan set to work traveling throughout Monroe and Ontario counties to deliver her lecture, "Is It a Crime for a Citizen of the U.S. to Vote?" She hoped to persuade possible jurors to accept her argument that women indeed had the right to vote under the Fourteenth Amendment. Her message must have gotten through, because the prosecution, fearing that no neutral jurors could be found, petitioned and received its request to move Susan's trial to the U.S. Circuit Court in Canandaigua, New York.

On June 17, 1873, Susan, wearing a simple silk dress and blue bonnet with a dotted veil, appeared in court before a jury of twelve white men. Judge Ward Hunt was presiding. Judge Hunt did not let Susan testify. He declared her incompetent as a witness because she was a woman. After the prosecution and defense presented their cases, Judge Hunt read his opinion—the one he had prepared before the trial had even begun. Judge Hunt then directed the jury to find Susan guilty.

Not until after the jury disclosed their verdict did Judge Hunt ask Susan if she had anything to say. The courtroom filled with "sublime silence" as Susan rose and replied: "Yes, your honor, I have many things to say; for in your ordered verdict of guilty you have trampled under foot every vital principle of our government. My natural rights, my civil rights, my political rights, my judicial rights, are all alike ignored. Robbed of the fundamental privilege of citizenship, I am degraded from the status of a citizen to that of a subject . . ."

Susan called her trial "[t]he greatest outrage History ever witnessed." Judge Hunt fined her $100, which she refused to pay. Judge Hunt did not order Susan imprisoned for failure to pay her fine because he knew that to imprison Susan would have given her the right to an appeal to the Supreme Court and the possibility that the Court might rule in her favor. Judge Hunt's action forced Susan to continue her fight for women's suffrage on the lecture circuit.

Susan would have to wait several months before continuing her suffrage lecture tour. Guelma, her older sister, was terminally ill with tuberculosis. Susan and Guelma's sisterly devotion to one another, so strong during their youth, had weathered the difficulties associated with different paths their respective lives had taken. Guelma had supported Susan's activism and had even left her sickbed to join Susan and her sisters to register and vote in the 1872 election.

Thus, when her trial ended, Susan joined Hannah and Mary at Guelma's bedside to nurse her. After several months, Guelma died on November 6, 1873. Susan

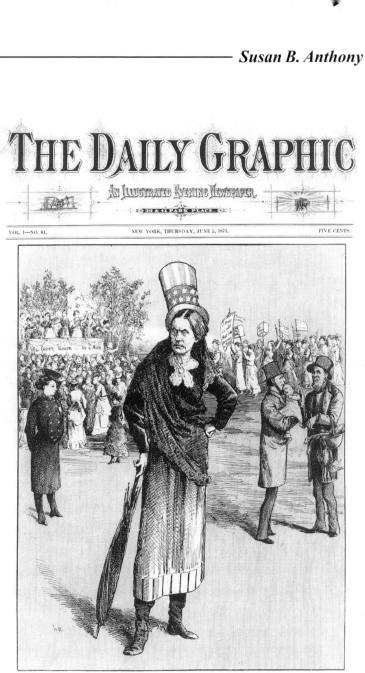

This caricature entitled "The Woman Who Dared" portrayed Susan B. Anthony after she had cast her ballot in the 1872 election. She was later arrested for her actions. *(Courtesy of the Library of Congress.)*

felt deeply saddened. To cope with her grief, Susan again turned to her work in much the same manner as she had done after her father's death.

Thanksgiving Day 1873 gave Susan a much-needed boost. After dinner, her cousin Anson Lapham, whom Susan loved almost as much as her father, handed her some papers canceling her $4,000 debt to him. He had loaned her the money for *The Revolution*, and said to her when she could not find the words to express her gratitude: "I feel the money was well spent."

Considering that Susan had to pay for all lecture expenses (pamphlets, hall rentals, candles, travel costs) out of the minimal admission fees, Cousin Anson's cancellation of her debt was especially generous and meaningful. Susan wrote in her diary: "[H]is manner made me feel his respect for & confidence in me—& that is more to me than the wealth of the Indies."

On December 2, Susan, Mary, and Hannah quietly celebrated their mother's eightieth birthday with her. The unshakable sisterhood shared by the Anthony women represented a life source for each one of them. Susan and Mary would be at their mother's and Hannah's bedsides during the last days of their final illnesses. And, when the time came, Mary would be there to nurse Susan through hers. Soon, Susan's "sisterhood" would expand to include the younger women joining the suffrage cause.

These women became known as "Susan's Girls" and would form the close cadre of admiring workers whom

Susan would train as the next generation of suffrage leaders. Carrie Chapman Catt, Anna Howard Shaw, Rachel Foster Avery, and other young suffragists would call her "Aunt Susan," and she would call them her "nieces." They would become her "lieutenants" and she their "General," and they would share her friendship and devotion because they shared her passion for the cause and dedication to women's suffrage above all else.

Susan continued her lecture tour throughout 1874 in spite of the negative impact on the movement from the Beecher-Tilton scandal. In 1875, Susan and the NWSA leaders were forced to abandon the "New Departure" strategy when the Supreme Court issued its *Minor v Happersett* decision. The Court ruled that states held the right to define "the privileges and immunities of citizens." Now the fight for women's suffrage would have to either be won on a state-by-state basis or through an amendment to the Constitution of the United States.

The suffrage battle received huge reinforcements with the election of Frances Willard as president of the Woman's Christian Temperance Union (WCTU). A close friend of Susan's, Frances Willard believed that women needed the power to elect legislators who would enact sweeping anti-alcohol changes to help them protect their homes, children, selves, and communities from the ravages of alcoholism. Willard called it the Home Protection Program.

The WCTU's involvement proved to be a double-edged sword. While it brought women into the movement, it also brought out the opposition. Tavern owners and alcohol distributors joined forces with others to maintain the status quo. They were hugely successful, which caused some women's rights leaders to rethink future alliances with social and moral reform causes.

Susan finished paying off *The Revolution*'s $10,000 debt in 1875 but continued to lecture throughout Iowa, urging support of a bill to give women the right to vote and earning money for the cause. She spent time in Kansas caring for her brother Daniel, who had been shot by a rival publisher. She also suffered a deep loss after the death of her dear friend Lydia Mott.

Susan most often turned to Lydia in times of crises and despair. Lydia supported Susan with her unbending conviction that regardless of the setback, progress was being made. In one of Susan's letters to Lydia she expressed her sentiments: "How you have compelled me to feel myself competent to go forward when trembling with doubt and distrust. I never can express the magnitude of my indebtedness to you."

The one-hundredth anniversary of the founding of the United States was commemorated in 1876. Susan and Elizabeth, joined by Matilda Joslyn Gage, the 1875 president of NWSA, set to work on a manifesto for the country's centenary celebration. They titled it the Declaration of the Rights of Women. In a firm, steady voice, Susan delivered the manifesto to a crowd at the Centennial Exposition held in Independence Square in Philadelphia on July 4: "And now, at the close of a hundred years . . . We ask of our rulers, at this hour, no special privileges, no special legislation. We ask justice, we ask equality, we ask that all civil and political rights that belong to citizens of the United States be guaranteed to us and our daughters forever."

That same year, one of Susan's dreams started to take shape. She had always wanted a permanent record of the women's rights and suffrage movements and had saved newspaper clippings, speeches, pamphlets, bills, sets of minutes, letters, petitions, and photographs ever since her father had first suggested she keep a scrapbook of notable events. Whom better to write it with than her close friend and partner, Elizabeth Cady Stanton?

Susan and Elizabeth spent years compiling the first volume of what would become a six-volume set called *History of Woman Suffrage*. Each volume would be approximately 1000 pages. Susan and Elizabeth, with some help from Matilda Joslyn Gage, compiled and edited Volume I, published in May 1881. Elizabeth would do the bulk of the work for Volume II, published in 1882, and Volume III, published in 1886. Susan and Ida Husted Harper would compile and edit Volume IV after Elizabeth's death, and Harper would compile and edit Volumes V and VI following Susan's death. Though biased to some degree, *History of Woman Suffrage* is still considered the most accurate history of the women's rights movement from 1848 to 1920.

Elizabeth Cady Stanton's daughter Margaret described one of Susan and Elizabeth's typical writing sessions:

> In the center of a large room, 20 by 22, with an immense bay window, hard wood floor and open fire, beside a substantial office desk with innumerable drawers and doors, filed with documents,— there sit our historians, surrounded with manuscripts and letters from Maine to Louisiana . . . They start off pretty well in the morning, fresh and amiable. They write page after page with alacrity, they laugh and talk, poke the fire by turn, and admire the flowers I place on their desk each morning. Everything is harmonious for a season, but after straining their eyes over the most illegible, disorderly manuscripts I ever beheld, suddenly the sky is overspread with dark and threatening clouds, and from the adjoining room I hear a hot dispute about something . . . Sometimes these disputes run so high that down go the pens, one sails out of one door and one out of the other, walking in opposite directions around the estate, and just as I have made up my mind that this beautiful friendship of forty years has at last terminated, I see them walking down the hill, arm in arm . . . When they return they go straight to work where they left off, as if nothing happened.

Susan sat by her younger sister Hannah's side when

Together, Elizabeth Cady Stanton and Susan B. Anthony wrote *History of Woman Suffrage*. *(Courtesy of the Library of Congress.)*

she died of tuberculosis in May 1877. This time, Susan's grief was almost inconsolable. Afraid that she, too, might succumb to the awful disease, Susan felt alone after having lost the two sisters with whom she was most close in age and lifetime memories. Susan turned to the Colorado Territory suffrage campaign for solace, setting aside her work on *History of Woman Suffrage* for the time being. As always, the stimulation of work consumed her thoughts and eventually eased her pain.

Susan called the Colorado campaign the most grueling of her career in 1877. As a rough, barely settled wilderness, canvassing the state was extremely taxing. Additionally, the men to whom Susan spoke were mostly immigrants, so they either did not understand what she was saying or became hostile to the idea of women's suffrage given their own lack of rights. The Colorado campaign answered for Susan whether suffrage should be pursued on a state-by-state basis or through a constitutional amendment. The latter seemed more effective and efficient.

On January 10, 1878, while Susan was lecturing in the West, the Honorable A.A. Sargent, Senator from California, submitted a joint resolution formally proposing to Congress a Sixteenth Amendment. It was the same amendment written by Elizabeth Cady Stanton ten years previous, and it read: "The right of citizens to vote shall not be denied or abridged by the United States or by any State on account of sex." It was referred to the Committee on Privileges and Elections where Elizabeth and other NWSA leaders spoke in its favor. Many petitions, speeches, and letters were written in favor of the amendment, yet, on June 14, 1878, Senator Wadleigh presented the committee's report:

> This proposed amendment forbids the United States, or any State to deny or abridge the right to vote on account of sex. If adopted, it will make several millions of female voters, totally inexperienced in political affairs, quite generally dependent upon the other sex, all incapable of performing military duty and without the power to enforce the laws which their numerical strength may enable them to make, and comparatively very few of whom wish to assume the irksome and responsible political duties which this measure thrusts upon them. An experiment so novel, a change so great, should only be made slowly and in response to a general public demand, of the existence of which there is no evidence before your committee.

After the amendment failed in 1878, Susan and suffragist leaders vowed to organize annual conventions in Washington, D. C., to reintroduce the amendment to Congress. These conventions generally took place in January or February, coinciding with legislative sessions and enabling suffragists to lobby their legislators and attend congressional hearings. These conventions would continue for over forty years.

Susan's mother died in 1880 at the age of eighty-six. Lucy left her home to Mary, who had devoted her life to her care and well-being. Susan had only spent extended visits in the red bricked house, stuffed with Victorian furniture, at 17 Madison Street. Her travels for suffrage would not allow her to settle in more permanently until 1891.

In 1882, disturbed by the increasing conservatism of NWSA and the narrowing of its focus to suffrage, Elizabeth Cady Stanton set sail for Europe. Elizabeth could not understand the willingness of women to accept oppression in the home and society in exchange for suffrage. Elizabeth felt that until society changed its beliefs and attitudes about a woman and "her place," the right to vote would have little effect on a woman's actual rights. A woman might be able to vote, she argued, but if society's religious bigotry did not sanction her right to a happy marriage, equal to a man's, then what good did her vote do her? Susan disagreed with Elizabeth, saying, "[Y]ou will have to keep pegging away, saying, 'Get rid of religious bigotry and then get political rights'; while I shall keep pegging away, saying 'Get political rights first and religious bigotry will melt like dew before the morning sun.' "

Elizabeth would stay in Europe on and off for the next nine years, virtually removing herself from the active campaign for women's suffrage. Instead, she would focus on her broader platform, issuing many controversial opinions on marriage, liberal divorce laws,

The Susan B. Anthony House at 17 Madison Street, Rochester, NY, is now a national landmark historic museum. *(Courtesy of the Library of Congress.)*

reproductive choice, and religious bigotry in letters, speeches, and articles. Many leaders tried to distance themselves and the suffrage movement from Elizabeth, fearing her radical ideas would harm their cause. Susan, however, remained loyal and defensive of her controversial friend.

Chapter Eight

"Failure is Impossible!"

As her friend Elizabeth set sail for Europe, Susan headed to Nebraska to help her most cherished "niece," Rachel Foster Avery, lead the suffrage campaign that was taking shape there. Thirty-nine years younger than Susan, Rachel impressed Susan with her executive capabilities and zeal and had distinguished herself as secretary for NWSA since 1880. Susan saw in Rachel the young "lieutenant" she wanted to take her place in the movement.

When Rachel married in the late 1880s, Susan was crushed. She became even more demanding of her other "lieutenants," trying to groom one to be like her. Susan expected her replacement to be as willing as she herself had been to forgo money, a home, marriage, personal time, food, sleep—even health—for the suffrage cause.

After the suffrage campaign failed in Nebraska, Rachel asked Susan to be her chaperone on a trip to Europe in 1883. Deciding that they would visit with Elizabeth Cady Stanton in England, Susan agreed.

In Europe, Susan, Rachel, and Elizabeth made many acquaintances and friendships with the leaders of women's rights movements in other countries. The trip, which lasted nine months, changed Susan's opinion that victory lay around the corner. As she listened to the trials and tribulations of the European women's rights movements, she seemed to resign herself to the idea that more slow, methodical work would be required to affect the changes she was seeking. Wanting to capitalize on what they had learned from the experiences of these European feminists, Susan and Elizabeth began talking about organizing an International Council of Women.

During this European trip, Susan first donned the dark garnet, velvet dress, ordered at Rachel's insistence in London, that would become her uniform for all future state and formal occasions. For most other occasions, Susan always wore a black silk dress and her distinctive red shawl of "silk crepe of exquisite fineness, with long, heavy, knotted fringe." One reporter described her shawl as "the oriflamme of [the] suffrage battle."

Susan would add other distinctive symbols to represent the suffrage cause. Yellow would become the official suffrage color, chosen for the sunflower of Colorado, where women first got the right to vote. Roses, a favorite flower of Susan's, became another symbol of the movement in memory of Susan's mother who had planted yellow rose bushes around her home.

Susan's attention to detail when planning a convention became legendary. She had the stage decorated to resemble a living room in order to appear more ladylike. Susan would dictate that rugs be placed on the floor and that a sofa, plump chairs, table, and lectern be arranged on the stage. Potted plants, flowers, portraits or busts of favorite suffrage leaders also had a place.

The walls would be lined with suffrage slogans and banners, and all of the delegates would wear yellow badges and ribbons. Even the flag used was symbolic of the suffrage cause. Its field of blue only held stars for those states that gave women the vote. Until passage of the Nineteenth Amendment, only four stars would appear on the suffragist flag—one for Wyoming, Utah, Colorado, and Idaho.

When Susan returned from Europe, she continued her annual addresses to congressional committees, urging their passage of the Sixteenth Amendment. Under her leadership, the NWSA had successfully lobbied Congress to appoint a Select Committee on Woman Suffrage. In 1884, Susan started planning for the first International Council of Women (ICW) to be held in Washington, D. C., in 1888. That year was chosen to commemorate the fortieth anniversary of the Seneca Falls Convention—the birth of the American women's rights movement.

When the ICW convened at Arbaugh's Opera House in Washington D.C., on March 25 for eight days, thousands of men and women attended over the course of the convention. Delegates representing a total of fifty-three women's organizations from England, India, Ireland, France, Norway, India, and the United States were in attendance, as well as representatives of trade unions, temperance groups, literary clubs, benevolent societies, and professional organizations.

More importantly for the women's movement were the people who shared the ICW stage with Susan and Elizabeth. Lucy Stone, Frederick Douglass, and other leaders of the AWSA joined them. Lucy Stone and Susan B. Anthony had actually met in December 1887 to discuss a possible merger of the AWSA and the NWSA.

Over two more years of negotiations would pass before the two organizations would finally unite to form the National American Woman Suffrage Association (NAWSA). Elizabeth Cady Stanton was then elected president, with Susan's wholehearted support, in recognition of her years of leadership in the fight for women's rights. Susan became vice-president-at-large.

Not only did the two organizations unite to form one association in 1890, but that same year, Susan B. Anthony celebrated her seventieth birthday. In her tribute to Susan, Elizabeth said, "If there is one part of my life that gives me more satisfaction than any other, it is my friendship of forty years' standing with Susan B. Anthony. Her heroism, faithfulness and conscientious devotion to what she thinks her duty has been a constant stimulus to me to thought and action. Ours has been indeed a friendship of hard work and self-denial . . ."

Pleased with the merger, Susan left for South Dakota for the state suffrage campaign. During this campaign, she became aware of the strong leadership potential of two of her "nieces," Carrie Chapman Catt and Anna Howard Shaw (later the Reverend Anna Howard Shaw). When the 1892 annual NAWSA convention met, they elected Susan president. Elizabeth Cady Stanton had resigned her presidency at that meeting after giving one of her most memorable speeches, "The Solitude of Self."

When the World's Congress of Representative Women (WCRW) opened their pavilion at the World's Fair in 1893, at the Chicago Art Palace, twenty-seven nations had representation. Susan, as president of NAWSA, had struggled to make the WCRW exhibit a success, wanting to showcase women's achievements as a part of the World's Fair. Only 10,000 people could be seated in the Art Palace, but 150,000 passed through the gates wanting to see the woman who inspired them, Susan B. Anthony.

That same year, Susan attended many of the political party conventions in hopes of convincing party leaders to add women's voting rights to their party platforms. It was a futile effort. She then directed her energies to managing her "lieutenant" Carrie Chapman Catt, who was in Colorado to head up their woman suffrage campaign. Colorado became the first state to enact women's suffrage by a popular referendum. Energized by this success, Susan spent the next year fighting for suffrage

Carrie Chapman Catt succeeded Anthony as president of NAWSA in 1900.
(Courtesy of the Library of Congress.)

in New York and Kansas. Neither effort proved successful.

Susan, Anna Howard Shaw, and several other "lieutenants" traveled to California in 1895 after the state's
legislative decision to submit a suffrage amendment to
its voters on the 1896 ballot. It became the most exten-
sively organized and largest suffrage campaign to date
with cooperation between the NAWSA, the WCTU, and
state suffragist organizations. The campaign ended in
another sad, miserable defeat, however. Not until 1911,
when the lobbying efforts of the liquor interests were
finally weakened, would a women's suffrage referendum pass in California by a slim 3,587 vote margin.
Even though suffrage failed in California in 1896,
NAWSA's campaign in Idaho succeeded.

In 1896, Susan appointed Ida Husted Harper to be
her authorized biographer. Together they worked
throughout 1897 to compile two volumes of her biography, *The Life and Work of Susan B. Anthony*, published
in 1898. Ida would finish and publish a third volume in
1908, after Susan's death.

Susan continued to represent NAWSA as its president throughout 1899. She attended the ICW in London, leading the U.S. delegation. Her speech in
Westminster Hall was greeted by a sea of waving, white
handkerchiefs, instead of the usual applause. This form
of greeting was called the Chautauqua salute and continued as a traditional form of welcome and approval at
women's rights conventions. One reporter described it

as "much more dignified than handclapping and stamping."

At the age of eighty, Susan B. Anthony resigned as the president of NAWSA in 1900 "because I want to see the organization in the hands of those who are to have its management in the future," she said. "I was elected secretary of a woman suffrage society in 1852, and from that day to this have held an office." Carrie Chapman Catt easily won election by a vote of 254 to twenty-four to be Susan's successor. As Susan turned over the gavel, she said: "Suffrage is no longer a theory, but an actual condition, and new conditions bring new duties. These new duties, these changed conditions, demand stronger hands, younger heads, and fresher hearts. In Mrs. Catt you have my ideal leader. I present to you my successor."

Moved by the significance of the proceedings, as many women were using their handkerchiefs on their eyes as were waving them in the air. Carrie Chapman Catt said quickly: "Your president, if you please, but Miss Anthony's successor, never! There is but one Miss Anthony, and she could not have a successor."

Though national women's suffrage had not been achieved, Susan could look back on the strides women had made with great pride. She reported that the most recent census showed that women had finally penetrated many professions, an achievement that would not have been possible without the women's rights movement.

There were 219 women coal miners, thirty-two wood

choppers, thirty quarry workers, fifty-nine blacksmiths, 129 butchers, 191 carpenters, four locomotive engineers and firemen, two veterinary surgeons, 4,555 women doctors, 208 lawyers, twenty-two architects, 337 dentists, 888 journalists, 1,235 clergywomen and 10,810 artists. "It is beyond a doubt that before long women will be sent to Congress as Representatives by some of the States . . . and who knows but that within the next century they may be appointed to the Supreme Bench? Indeed, it is not at all beyond the bounds of possibility that a woman may be elected President some day," Susan said.

Making the University of Rochester, located in her hometown, a co-educational institution became Susan's next project. The trustees promised her that if she raised $50,000 by September 8, 1900 for an endowment fund for women to study, the University would concede.

Susan felt confident that she had succeeded in raising the fund when she received a call from a trustee on September 7, informing her that an additional $8,000 was needed. Susan was obliged to go to her friends and family living in Rochester, all of whom had already given, as only twenty-four hours remained before the September 8 deadline. Her sister Mary gave $2,000, friends gave $2,000, and the pastor of a church gave $2,000.

With time running out, Susan pledged the cash value of her life insurance policy to complete the $8,000 balance. She had done it! Thanks to the efforts of Susan

B. Anthony, the first women to be admitted to the University of Rochester would graduate in 1904.

This victory did not come without cost, however. Susan suffered a stroke. She took several months to recover, though her inexhaustible energy never did return. She spent much of her recovery time in 1901 working with Ida Husted Harper on Volume IV of *History of Woman Suffrage*.

In June 1902, Susan stopped for a visit with her dear friend Elizabeth Cady Stanton, who was eighty-six years old. They both knew the end was near. When leaving, Susan embraced Elizabeth and began to weep. "Shall I see you again?" Elizabeth, composed, said, "Oh, yes, if not here, then in the hereafter, if there is one, and if there isn't we shall never know."

Susan's own views of religion were similar to her friend's. "I don't know what religion is," Susan said. "I only know what work is, and that is all I can speak on, this side of Jordan." That October, Susan wrote what would be her last letter to Elizabeth:

> My Dear Mrs. Stanton . . . We little dreamed when we began this contest, optimistic with the hope and buoyancy of youth, that half a century later we would be compelled to leave the finish of the battle to another generation of women . . . These strong young women will take our place and complete our work. There is an army of them, where we were but a handful . . . Ever lovingly yours, Susan B. Anthony.

Susan arrived back home in Rochester on a cold, crisp fall day, when she received the telegram from Stanton's daughter, which read, "Mother passed away at three o'clock. Harriot." Elizabeth Cady Stanton had died on October 26, 1902. The grief that Susan felt went far deeper than any she had experienced. It stunned her. Susan described her feelings in a letter to Ida Husted Harper: "It was an awful hush—it seems impossible—that the voice is hushed—that I have longed to hear for fifty years—longed to get her opinion of things—before I knew exactly where I stood—It is all at sea . . . What a world it is—it goes right on & on—no matter who lives or who dies!!"

In spite of her own poor health, Susan pressed on. "The hammer may as well fall one time as another," she said. Susan traveled abroad in 1904 to attend the ICW in Berlin, where she was introduced as "Miss Anthony of the World." One long time supporter said, "she was not only our Susan but everybody's." That same year, Susan and Mary were able to manage one final visit with their brother Daniel in Leavenworth, Kansas, just before he died, returning weeks later for his funeral.

Susan had to deal with the selection of a replacement for Carrie Chapman Catt that year as well. Catt was stepping down as president of NAWSA to care for her ailing husband. Susan insisted that the Reverend Anna Howard Shaw, another of her favorite "nieces," take over. Susan knew that Shaw could lead the organization, but that she would have to remain ever strong to withstand the criticism. To bolster Shaw, Susan explained her own philosophy of life: "No matter what is done or is not done, how you are criticized or misunderstood, or what efforts are made to block your path, remember that the only fear you need have is the fear of not standing by the thing you believe to be right. Take your stand and hold it: then let come what will, and receive the blows like a good soldier."

While maintaining an unbelievable schedule—even for someone half her age—Susan also traveled to eighteen states during her "retirement" years (1900-1906). She crossed the country to attend the 1905 NAWSA convention held in Oregon. While talking to a reporter on her cross-country trek, Susan gave her opinion against medical advice: "Oh, these doctors. They said I couldn't make the trip and live . . . and I sat and watched myself all the time expecting to die every minute; but I didn't."

Susan desperately wanted to attend the February 1906 NAWSA convention in Baltimore. In a raging blizzard, Mary, quite ill herself, prepared for the trip by train, wrapping Susan in mountains of blankets. By the time they reached the convention, Susan had a terrible cold and was forced to take bed rest.

She managed to rally for what would be her final speech. The applause and ovation lasted for ten minutes as the entire audience rose, waving their white handkerchiefs, many with tears streaming down their cheeks for they knew that this might be her last convention.

With superhuman strength, Susan went on to attend her eighty-sixth birthday celebration at the Church of Our Fathers at Thirteenth and L Streets in Washington, D. C. The widespread praise came from every sector. Even President Theodore Roosevelt sent his congratulations, to which Susan replied with a half-smile: "I would rather have him say a word to Congress for the cause than to praise me endlessly." The audience was delighted and responded wildly. Then Susan gave her final message: "There have been others also just as true and devoted to the cause—I wish I could name every one—but with such women consecrating their lives, failure is impossible!"

Two days later, Susan B. Anthony lay bedridden with pneumonia and a failing heart. Friends and family were at a loss to fathom what their lives would be like without her. When Susan peacefully passed away at 12:40 a.m. on March 13, 1906, Mary was combing her hair and the Reverend Anna Howard Shaw was holding her hand.

Ten thousand mourners passed by Susan's casket as it laid in state in the Central Presbyterian Church in Rochester, guarded by twelve women dressed in white. Susan was dressed in her traditional black silk dress. A jeweled pin of an American flag with only four tiny diamonds, representing the stars of the suffrage states, was pinned to her dress. After the mourners had passed, the pin was removed and given to the Reverend Shaw. Susan's casket was then closed for the last time.

Twenty-five hundred mourners braved the fierce snowstorm to accompany her body to Mount Hope Cemetery. Women students from the University of Rochester, wearing their black academic gowns and mortarboards, carried the flowers as honor bearers, leading the funeral procession.

Reverend Shaw delivered the final address:

> The world is profoundly stirred by the loss of our great General, and in consequence the lukewarm are becoming zealous, the prejudiced are disarming and the suffragists are renewing their vows of fidelity to the cause for which Miss Anthony lived and died. Her talismanic words, the last she ever uttered before a public audience, 'Failure is impossible,' shall be inscribed on our banner and engraved in our hearts.

And there beneath a simple white headstone, Susan B. Anthony was laid to rest. Written by Susan herself, her epitaph speaks volumes about the person she was: "When it is a funeral, remember that I want there should be no tears. Pass on, and go on with the work."

Sources

CHAPTER ONE: A Quaker Upbringing

p. 9, "less eager to enter that condition . . ." Miriam Gurko, *The Ladies of Seneca Falls, The Birth of the Woman's Rights Movement* (New York: Schocken Books, 1976), 110.

p. 10, "the very being or legal existence . . ." Kathleen Barry, *Susan B. Anthony: A Biography of A Singular Feminist* (1stBooks Library, Rev. 2000), 10.

p. 14, "What an absurd notion..." Gurko, *The Ladies of Seneca Falls*, 109.

p. 15, "the pleasure of viewing the dust from . . ." Barbara Weisberg, *Susan B. Anthony* (Philadelphia: Chelsea House Publishers, 1988), 31.

CHAPTER TWO: Headmistress

p. 17, "Did a large washing today . . ." Katharine Anthony, *Susan B. Anthony: Her Personal History and Her Era* (Garden City, NY: Doubleday & Co., Inc., 1954) 58.

p. 18, "My feelings are inexpressible . . ." Barry, *Singular Feminist*, 37.

p. 19, "Did you ever whip any of your . . ." Lynn Sheer, *Failure is Impossible: Susan B. Anthony in Her Own Words* (New York: Random House, Times Books, 1995), 207.

p. 19, "In the true marriage relation . . ." Ibid., 10.

p. 20, "Joseph had a headache . . ." Ibid., 6.

p. 20, "found he [the doctor] had cut . . ." Katharine Anthony, *Susan B. Anthony, Her Personal History*, 67.

p. 21, "It is with great sorrow . . ."Ibid., 70.

p. 22, "You must miss the society . . ." Barry, *Singular Feminist*, 44.

p. 24, "My fancy for attending dances . . ." Sheer, *Failure is Impossible*, xx.

p. 28, "If we say we love the cause . . ." Geoffrey C.Ward, *Not for Ourselves Alone: The Story of Elizabeth Cady Stanton and Susan B. Anthony* (New York: Alfred A. Knoph, 1999), 46.

CHAPTER THREE: Temperance Reform

p. 29, "the smartest woman that was . . ." Ward, *Not for Ourselves Alone*, 47.

p. 32, "I pray every single second . . ." Judith E. Harper, *Susan B. Anthony: A Biographical Companion* (Santa Barbara, CA: ABC-CLIO, Inc., 1998), 164.

p. 32, "Shall I tell a man . . ." Weisberg, *Susan B. Anthony*, 40.

p. 36, "The sisters were not invited . . ." Ibid., 42.

p. 38, "I went home to my old Quaker . . ." Sheer, *Failure is Impossible*, xx-xxi.

p. 40, "the right which woman . . ." Ward, *Not for Ourselves Alone*, 68.

p. 41, "let the past be past . . ." Ibid., 72.

CHAPTER FOUR: Women's Rights and Abolition

p. 42, "Thus as I passed from . . ." ed. Ann D. Gordon, *The Selected Papers of Elizabeth Cady Stanton and Susan B. Anthony, Volume I, In the School of Anti-Slavery 1840-1866* (New Brunswick, NJ: Rutgers Univ. Press, 1998), 230.

P. 43, "We know that God created . . ." Weisberg, *Susan B. Anthony*, 55.

p. 46, "It is the depriving of . . ." Harper, *Biographical Companion,* 277.

p. 50, "from the time of Moses . . ." Ward, *Not for Ourselves Alone*, 92.

p. 52, "You would die before . . ." Harper, *Biographical Companion*, 100.

CHAPTER FIVE: Civil War and Reconstruction
p. 54, "Do with them precisely . . ." Sheer, *Failure is Impossible*, 33.

p. 55, "[S]uperintended the plowing . . ." Ibid., 33.

p. 55, "[I]t seemed to me the . . ." Harper, *Biographical Companion*, 31.

p. 56, "Forget conventionalisms; . . ." Sheer, *Failure is Impossible*, 35.

p. 61, "This is a critical . . ." Ibid., 38.

CHAPTER SIX: The Women's Rights Movement Divides
p. 68, "Fiftieth birthday! . . ." Sheer, *Failure is Impossible*, xvi.

p. 68, "My pride for women . . ." Ward, *Not for Ourselves Alone*, 134.

p. 68, "We feel that our present . . ." Sheer, *Failure is Impossible*, 180.

p. 69, "I was entirely won by . . ." Harper, *Biographical Companion*, 32.

p. 69, "She does not wait . . ." Sheer, *Failure is Impossible*, xxiv.

p. 70, "I have done without . . ." Ibid., 227.

p. 71, "She has carried on more campaigns . . ." Ibid., 228.

p. 73, "I don't believe it . . ." Ibid., 63.

p. 73, ". . . on way home, Rochester, N.Y . . . ." ed. Ann D. Gordon, *The Selected Papers of Elizabeth Cady Stanton and Susan B. Anthony, Volume II, Against an Aristocracy of Sex, 1866 to 1873* (New Brunswick, NJ: Rutgers Univ. Press, 2000), 463.

p. 73, "Miss Anthony . . . was generally . . ." Sheer, *Failure is Impossible*, 241.

p. 75, "I never was so hurt . . ." Ward, *Not for Ourselves Alone*, 141.

CHAPTER SEVEN: Woman Suffrage above All Else!
p. 78, "Yes, your honor . . ." Barry, *Singular Feminist*, 304.
p. 78, "[t]he greatest outrage . . ." Sheer, *Failure is Impossible*, 109.
p. 80, "I feel the money was . . ." Barry, *Singular Feminsit*, 308.
p. 80, "[H]is manner made me feel . . ." Ibid., 308.
p. 82, "How you have compelled . . ." Harper, *Biographical Companion*, 133.
p. 83, "And now, at the close of . . ." ed. Marjorie Spruill, *One Woman, One Vote: Rediscovering the Woman Suffrage Movement.* (Troutdale, OR: New Sage Press, 1995), 36.
p. 84, "In the center . . ." Sheer, *Failure is Impossible*, 286-287.
p. 87, "This proposed amendment . . ." eds. Elizabeth Cady Stanton, Susan B. Anthony and Matilda Joslyn Gage, *History of Woman Suffrage, Volume III, 1876-1885.* Reprint Edition, (Salem, NH: Ayer Company Publishers, Inc., 1985), 112.
p. 88, "[Y]ou will have to keep . . ." Barry, *Singular Feminist*, 347.

CHAPTER EIGHT: "Failure is Impossible!"
p. 93, "If there is one part . . ." Sheer, *Failure is Impossible*, 173.
p. 97, "because I want to see . . ." David K. Boynick, *Women Who Led the Way: Eight Pioneers for Equal Rights* (New York: Thomas Y. Crowell Co., 1959), 56.
p. 97, "I was elected . . ." Sheer, *Failure is Impossible*, 70.
p. 97, "Suffrage is no longer a theory . . ." Ibid., 320-321.
p. 97, "Your president, if you please . . ." Ibid., 321.
p. 99, "Shall I see you again? . . ." Barry, *Singular Feminist*, 365.
p. 99, "I don't know what . . ." Sheer, *Failure is Impossible*, 247.
p. 99, "My Dear Mrs. Stanton . . ." Ibid., 175.
p. 100, "It was an awful . . ." Barry, *Singular Feminist*, 366-67.
p. 101, "No matter what . . ." Harper, *Biographical Companion,* 34.
p. 101, "Oh, these doctors . . ." Ibid., 205.
p. 102, "There have been . . ." Sheer, *Failure is Impossible*, 324.
p. 103, "The world is profoundly stirred . . ." Ibid., 326.
p. 103, "When it is a funeral . . ." Ibid., 327.

Bibliography

Anthony, Katharine. *Susan B. Anthony: Her Personal History and Her Era.* Garden City, NY: Doubleday & Company, Inc., 1954.

Anthony, Susan B. Anthony and Ida Husted Harper, Eds. *History of Woman Suffrage, Volume 4, 1883-1900.* Salem, NH: Ayer Company, Publishers, Inc., Reprint Ed. 1985.

Barry, Kathleen. *Susan B. Anthony: A Biography of a Singular Feminist.* 1st Books Library, 2000.

Bolton, Sarah K. *Lives of Girls Who Became Famous.* New York: Thomas Y. Crowell Co., 1949.

Boynick, David K. *Women Who Led the Way: Eight Pioneers for Equal Rights.* New York: Thomas Y. Crowell Co., 1959.

DuBois, Ellen Carol. *The Elizabeth Cady Stanton—Susan B. Anthony Reader: Correspondence, Writings, Speeches.* Boston, Northeastern Un. Press, Revised Ed., 1992.

Gordon, Ann D., Ed. *The Selected Papers of Elizabeth Cady Stanton & Susan B. Anthony, Vol. I: In the School of Anti-Slavery, 1840-1866.* New Brunswick, NJ: Rutgers Un. Press, 1998.

———. *The Selected Papers of Elizabeth Cady Stanton & Susan B. Anthony, Vol. II: Against an Aristocracy of Sex, 1866-1873.* New Brunswick, NJ: Rutgers Un. Press, 2000.

Gurko, Miriam. *The Ladies of Seneca Falls: The Birth of the Woman's Rights Movement.* New York: Schocken Books, 1976.

Harper, Ida Husted, Ed. *History of Woman Suffrage, Volume 5, 1900-1920.* Salem, NH: Ayer Company, Publishers, Inc., Reprint Ed. 1985.

———. *History of Woman Suffrage, Volume 6, 1900-1920.*

Salem, NH: Ayer Company, Publishers, Inc., Reprint Ed. 1985.

Harper, Judith E. *Susan B. Anthony: A Biographical Companion.* Santa Barbara, CA: ABC-CLIO, Inc., 1998.

Nathan, Dorothy. *Women of Courage.* New York: Random House, 1964.

Sheer, Lynn. *Failure is Impossible: Susan B. Anthony in Her Own Words.* New York: Times Books, Random House,1995.

Stanton, Elizabeth Cady and Susan B. Anthony and Matilda Joslyn Gage, Eds. *History of Woman Suffrage, Volume 1, 1848-1861.* Salem, NH: Ayer Company, Publishers, Inc., Reprint Ed. 1985.

————. *History of Woman Suffrage, Volume 2, 1861-1876.* Salem, NH: Ayer Company, Publishers, Inc., Reprint Ed. 1985.

————. *History of Woman Suffrage, Volume 3, 1876-1885.* Salem, NH: Ayer Company, Publishers, Inc., Reprint Ed., 1985.

Ward, Geoffry. *Not For Ourselves Alone: The Story of Elizabeth Cady Stanton and Susan B. Anthony.* New York: Alfred A. Knopf, 1999.

Weisberg, Barbara. *Susan B. Anthony.* Philadelphia: Chelsea House Publishers,1988.

Wheeler, Marjorie Spruill, Ed. *One Woman, One Vote: Rediscovering the Woman Suffrage Movement.* Troutdale, OR: New Sage Press, 1995.

Susan B. Anthony Websites

The Susan B. Anthony House National Historic Landmark Museum: *www.susanbanthonyhouse.org*

The Huntington Library, Art Collections, and Botanical Gardens, Votes for Women Online Exhibit: *www.huntington.org/vfw/index.html*

The History Place Great Speeches Collection, Susan B. Anthony on Women's Right to Vote: *www.historyplaces.com/speeches/anthony.htm*

Index

A. A. Sargent, 86
American Anti-Slavery Society (AASS), 57
American Equal Rights Association (AERA), 60-62, 65, 67
American Woman Suffrage Association (AWSA), 67, 75, 93
Anthony, Daniel, 9-10, 12-18, 20- 22, 25, 29, 38, 55
Anthony, Daniel (brother), 11, 58, 82, 100
Anthony, Eliza, 11
Anthony, Hannah, 9-11, 21-22, 74, 76, 78, 80, 84
Anthony, Jacob Merritt, 11
Anthony, Lucy Reed, 9-10, 12, 22, 25, 29, 88
Anthony, Mary, 11, 25, 76, 78, 80, 88, 98, 100-101
Anthony, Susan Brownell, and abolition, 31-33, 46-47, 49, 53-57, 59-62, 66-67
    biography, 96
    childhood, 9-13

death, 102
education, 12, 14-15, 17
funeral, 102-103
legacy, 9, 15, 103
and marriage, 17, 19-20
as teacher, 13, 18-19, 23-25, 29
and temperance, 28-30, 34, 36-38 , 40-42, 81-82
and voting, 76-78
Anthony, Susannah Brownell, 10
Aurora Leigh, 74
Avery, Rachel Foster, 81, 90-91

Beecher, Henry Ward, 75
Blackwell,Antionette (Brown), 38, 45, 50, 60
Blackwell, Henry, 62, 67
Bloomer, Amelia, 33, 37
Brown, John, 48-49
Brown, Mary, 49, *51*
Browning, Elizabeth Barrett, 74